Nonfiction Comprehension

GRADES 5-6

S0-AGI-726

Reading Strategies for the Content Areas

Nonfiction Comprehension: Grades 5–6, SV 8948-6

Students learn much about their world through reading. Fiction, through illustration, tells them about people and human nature. Nonfiction, through information, tells them what the world is like. Just as certain skills are needed to gain a deeper understanding of fiction, so are certain skills needed to gain the most from nonfiction. The purpose of this book is to help teachers to pass on those nonfiction skills to young readers so they can move from learning to read to reading to learn.

As students progress through the grades, their reading load increases and changes. Students may encounter an increased volume of text. They may have to deal with new vocabulary and new concepts in each content area. They may lack prior knowledge to apply to new information. They may have a basic unfamiliarity with expository text features. They may be asked to show their understanding of nonfiction selections on standardized tests. This book includes reading selections and techniques to help teachers to overcome these common hurdles that students face.

This book is especially appropriate for:

- Reading teachers who want to provide extra nonfiction practice using specific comprehension skills;

- Teachers in other disciplines who want to reinforce content-specific comprehension skills;

- Parents who want to provide extra nonfiction reading practice for their child.

A **good reader** is a **good learner.** The goal of this book is to **make all students good readers!**

 Use and Organization

Research suggests that "explicit teaching techniques are particularly effective for comprehension strategy instruction. In explicit instruction, teachers tell readers why and when they should use strategies, what strategies they should use, and how to apply them. The steps of explicit instruction typically include direct explanation, teacher modeling ("thinking aloud"), guided practice, and application." (*Put Reading First*, p. 53)

This book includes two types of teacher information pages. The book is divided into six units that identify major comprehension areas. These units are further divided into 16 specific comprehension skills. At the beginning of each unit is a teacher information page that identifies the comprehension skills in that unit and provides background details and recognition strategies for each skill. Each comprehension skill is then covered in a lesson that includes reading selections from a variety of content areas. At the beginning of each lesson is another teaching information page that covers the reading selections in the lesson. Summaries of each selection are provided, along with vocabulary words and writing exercises. Included on this page are approaches to tap prior knowledge, emphasize and reinforce the comprehension skill, preview text features, and help students to comprehend the selection.

Each lesson contains one to three reading selections that emphasize a specific comprehension skill, such as summary or comparison-contrast. Many of the reading selections also contain visual aids that the student can use to gain extra information about the topic. A unit on visual aids prepares the student for the use of these tools. Each reading selection also includes activities that center on comprehension and vocabulary. At the back of the book are a complete answer key and a variety of graphic organizers.

TECHNIQUES

to Improve Comprehension

This book offers a variety of comprehension techniques on the teacher information pages. Here are more comprehension techniques that can be used to increase student comprehension.

- Introduce the reading skills of skimming and scanning. Skimming notes the general subject and major headings. Scanning looks for key words.

- Model a fluent reading process: read; stop and think; reread when comprehension breaks down.

- Ask questions that help relate the reading selection to the reader's experiences, emotions, or knowledge.

- Use comparison-contrast to help the students to connect new information to known information.

- Model and require students to create questions about their reading.

- Use graphic organizers to organize and display group thinking, questioning, and learning.

- Help the students to draw conclusions from information the author has provided. Help the students to question their way through the selection.

- Have the students summarize the main points of each selection or section of the reading.

- Provide ways for the students to record changes in their thinking as new information is gathered.

Bibliography

Armbruster, B. B., F. Lehr, and J. Osbourne. *Put Reading First: The Research Building Blocks for Teaching Children to Read.* Washington, D. C.: National Institute for Literacy, 2001.

Skill	Mathematics	Biography	History	Economics	Geography	Earth Science	Life Science	Physical Science	Daily Skills
Diagrams	7				61	61	8, 77	56, 93	93
Graphs	11, 12, 13		12, 13	11, 12	11, 13				
Charts and Time Lines			15, 18, 75, 91	17, 75		84			15, 75, 91
Maps			63, 105	21	20, 21, 63	63			
Main Idea		26			26, 27	27	25		
Details		35	34, 36			34	34, 35		
Summary		41	41				40		
Narration of Event		41, 46, 47	41, 46, 47, 49						
Narration of Process	55					54	54, 113	56	55, 113
Cause-Effect		59	60, 61		61	61	59		
Description		70	70		68	68	68, 69		
Division							77		
Classification				86		84	82		
Comparison-Contrast	7		13, 91	90			95	93	91, 93
Drawing Conclusions		99, 100	100, 101, 103		99, 100				
Fact or Opinion?						109	111, 113	110	110, 111, 113

Nonfiction Comprehension: Grades 5–6, SV 8948-6

UNIT 1 — Visual Aids

We all know the old saying, "A picture is worth a thousand words." The saying is true for visual aids, which includes graphic organizers. These graphic sources range from simple illustrations to complicated graphs and charts. Often, graphic sources such as diagrams, graphs, charts, and maps are skipped over by young readers because they look hard to understand. These visual aids are not hard to understand if students take the time to study them. These graphic sources can give more information in a smaller space than the written word.

• Diagrams (Lesson 1)

A diagram is an illustration that is meant to explain rather than represent. It does not try to show the reader what the thing looks like. Instead, it breaks the topic into its parts and arrangement. For example, a diagram of a food chain would show all the members of the chain. It would use arrows to show the arrangement or relationship between the members. Diagrams are very helpful in explaining mathematical or scientific topics.

To understand a diagram:
- Read the title of the diagram or article carefully. What is it about?
- Read all of the labels. Take time to figure out what they mean.
- If the diagram has a caption, read the caption carefully.
- If arrows are used in the diagram, study the movement suggested by the arrows.
- Try to identify all the parts and their relationship to one another.

• Graphs (Lesson 2)

A graph is a diagram that uses pictures, points, lines, bars, or areas to show and compare information. A pictograph uses pictures to show information. A bar graph uses bars, and a line graph uses one or more lines to give information. A pie graph uses slices of a round graph to show facts. Some graphs will have two lines or two bars to compare and contrast information. Sometimes students are asked to compare and contrast two graphs.

To understand a graph:
- First, identify the kind of graph.
- Read the title of the graph carefully. What information does the graph show?
- Read the labels on the graph. Take time to figure out what they mean.
- Follow the bars or lines with your finger.
- Move a finger from the labels to the point on the line or bar to get the information you need.
- If a graph uses pictures, be sure to check how much each picture represents.

• Charts and Time Lines (Lesson 3)

A chart presents exact information in an orderly way. Charts arrange facts in a way that makes them easy to read and understand. Often, charts include times or numbers. A flow chart helps to show the order of events. A time line shows the order of events along a vertical or horizontal line.

To understand a chart or time line:
- Read the title of the chart or time line carefully.
- Read all the labels in the chart or time line.
- Read the times or numbers in the chart or time line.
- Use your finger to follow the rows or columns of a chart, or the movement of the flowchart or time line.
- Be sure you know what information you need and what information the chart or time line gives.

• Maps (Lesson 4)

Maps are used to give information about a place. Maps are like a drawing of a place from above. Maps can tell about the boundaries of places. They can tell about the landscape, the climate, or the population. Most maps have the same features, such as a compass rose, a legend or key, and a distance scale.

To understand a map:
- Read the title of the map. What information does the map give?
- Find the compass rose. Run your finger along the points of the rose. Usually, north is toward the top of the map.
- Find the distance scale. Practice measuring a distance on the map.
- Find the legend or key. Look at all the symbols. Take time to figure out what they mean.
- Find some of the symbols on the map.
- Study the map to find the information you need.

LESSON 1

Diagrams

BEFORE READING

Tap Prior Knowledge

Ask the students how they keep their facts straight when they read nonfiction.

"Using Venn Diagrams": Suggest to the students that one good way to remember things is graphically. If they draw pictures of things, they can often remember that information longer. A Venn diagram is one way to organize information.

"An Ocean Food Chain": Ask the students if they have ever drawn a picture to give information. The pictorial diagram is another way to convey information.

Skill to Emphasize

Review the section about diagrams on page 5. Point out the diagrams in the selections.

DURING READING

Preview Text Features

Point out the diagrams in the articles. Point out the labels in the two diagrams. The labels give valuable information about the diagram. Point out the arrows in the food chain; they show the eating order. Boldfaced words indicate vocabulary words.

Comprehending the Selection

You may wish to model how to identify the main idea in each selection by asking: What is this article mostly about? Ask the students how the diagrams help them to learn more about the topic.

AFTER READING

Reinforce the Comprehension Skill

Remind the students that a diagram is an illustration that is meant to explain. It breaks the topic into its parts and arrangement. Ask the students how the diagrams in each selection show the parts and arrangement of the parts.

Assess

Have the students complete the activities for each selection.

WRITE ABOUT IT

Have the students draw a diagram that helps to explain a topic they have studied recently in science.

AT HOME

Have the students search through the newspaper or new magazines for diagrams and bring these diagrams to school to share with the class.

Using Venn Diagrams

The Oxwatch Weekly Farm Report found that of 200 farms in the area, 80 have only cows, 60 have only sheep, 40 have both, and 20 have neither. A math student decided to make a Venn diagram of this information, like the below. The section formed by the intersecting circles represents the farms with both cows and sheep. The area outside both circles represents farms with neither cows nor sheep.

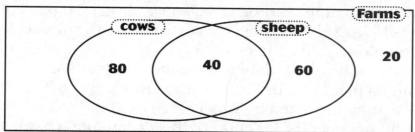

Fill in the Venn diagram below to show that half of the 200 farms have cows and sheep, 10 have no animals, and the number of farms that have only cows is the same as those that have only sheep. Then use your Venn diagram to answer the questions.

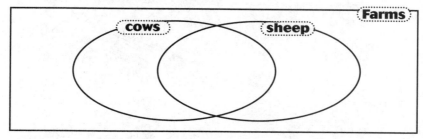

1. How many farms have cows? _____

2. How many farms have no sheep? _____

3. How many farms have animals? _____

Make a Venn diagram to show this information.

a. 175 farms have horses.
b. 100 farms have only pigs.
c. 75 farms have no animals, which is 50 more than have both.

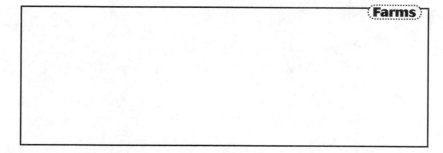

Nonfiction Comprehension: Grades 5–6, SV 8948-6

An Ocean Food Chain

Small living things are often the food for bigger living things. These bigger living things are the food for even larger living things. The way that different living things depend on each other for food is called a **food chain**. There are food chains in both land **environments** and water environments.

All food chains start with plants because plants make their own food. To make food, plants need water, minerals, carbon dioxide gas, and the energy of sunlight. Animals cannot make food. Animals must eat plants or other animals for their food.

In oceans, plant **plankton** make their own food. They are the beginning of one kind of ocean food chain. The plant plankton are food for water animals, such as animal plankton. Animal plankton, in turn, are the food for bigger water animals, such as shrimp. The shrimp are eaten by small fish. The small fish are food for larger fish. People who eat these larger fish are part of this ocean food chain, too.

All ocean food chains do not follow the same path. There are many different food chains in the ocean. But all food chains, on land and in water, begin with plants.

The diagram shows one kind of ocean food chain.

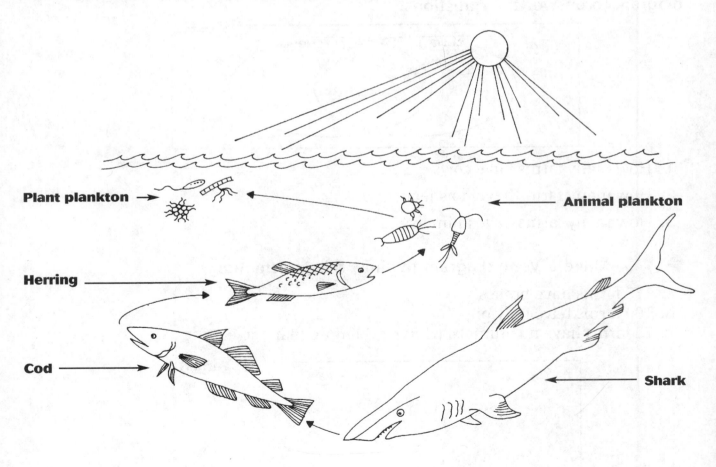

Name _____ Date_____

Comprehension and Vocabulary Review

➤ The living things listed below are part of an ocean food chain. Put them in the correct order. The first one is done for you.

1. _____ animal plankton

   _____ herring

   _____ shark

   ___1___ plant plankton

   _____ cod

   _____ people

➤ Darken the circle by the best answer.

1. The way that different living things depend on each other for food is called ____.
   Ⓐ an environment
   Ⓑ plankton
   Ⓒ a food chain
   Ⓓ herring

2. To make food, plants need water, minerals, carbon dioxide gas, and ____.
   Ⓐ fish
   Ⓑ sunlight
   Ⓒ plankton
   Ⓓ people

3. All food chains, on land and in water, begin with ____.
   Ⓐ large fish
   Ⓑ people
   Ⓒ grocery stores
   Ⓓ plants

4. In the ocean food chain, the larger fish are eaten by ____.
   Ⓐ plants
   Ⓑ people
   Ⓒ plankton
   Ⓓ minerals

➤ Write a complete sentence to answer the question.

5. Why do all food chains start with plants? _____

_____

_____

Nonfiction Comprehension: Grades 5–6, SV 8948-6

Graphs

BEFORE READING

Tap Prior Knowledge

"Puerto Rico Exports": Ask the students if they know how many products they use each day that come from other countries.

"North and South in the Civil War": Ask the students what they think would help a country to win a war.

"Population of the North and South in 1860": Ask the students if they know the ethnic makeup of their community.

Skill to Emphasize

Review the section about graphs on page 5. Point out the graphs in the selections.

DURING READING

Preview Text Features

Point out that the graph in "Puerto Rico Exports" uses pictures to represent the crops exported from Puerto Rico. Each picture stands for a certain amount of money. The graph in "North and South in the Civil War" uses bars to compare the relative strength of the two sides in the Civil War in 1861. The two circle graphs in "Population of the North and South in 1860" compare the populations of the North and the South in 1860. Boldfaced words indicate vocabulary words.

Comprehending the Selection

Ask the students: *What does each graph show?* Ask the students how the graphs help them to learn more about the topic.

AFTER READING

Reinforce the Comprehension Skill

Remind the students that a graph can use pictures, bars, or slices of a circle to show and compare information. Ask the students if they think graphs are a good way to show information.

Assess

Have the students complete the activities for each selection.

WRITE ABOUT IT

Have the students draw a bar graph that compares the number of boys and girls in their class.

AT HOME

Have the students search through the newspaper or news magazines for graphs and bring these graphs to school to share with the class.

SELECTION DETAILS

Summary

"Puerto Rico Exports" (page 11): This article uses a pictograph to illustrate the major crop exports of Puerto Rico.

"North and South in the Civil War" (page 12): This article uses a double bar graph to illustrate the key details about the two sides in the American Civil War.

"Population of the North and South in 1860" (page 13): The two circle graphs compare the populations of the two sides in the American Civil War in 1860.

Selection Type

Social Studies Articles

Comprehension Skill

Use Visual Aids for Information

Standards

Reading
- Use a variety of appropriate reference materials, including representations of information such as diagrams, maps, and charts, to gather information.

Social Studies
- Explain why and how countries trade goods and services.
- Analyze the events of North vs. South during the expansion of the nation.

VOCABULARY

Introduce the vocabulary words. Write the words on the board. Help students find a definition for each word. Have students use each word in a sentence.

"Puerto Rico Exports"
climate   exported

"Population of the North and South in 1860"
percent   population

Name _____ Date_____

Puerto Rico Exports

Puerto Rico grows many different crops. The mild **climate** of Puerto Rico helps these crops to grow well. Many of these products are **exported** from Puerto Rico to other countries. The graph below shows some of the crops exported from Puerto Rico.

CROPS EXPORTED FROM PUERTO RICO

☕	Coffee	☕	☕	☕	☕	☕	☕
🎋	Sugar Cane	🎋	🎋	🎋			
🍌	Plantains	🍌	🍌	🍌	🍌		
🍍	Pineapples	🍍					

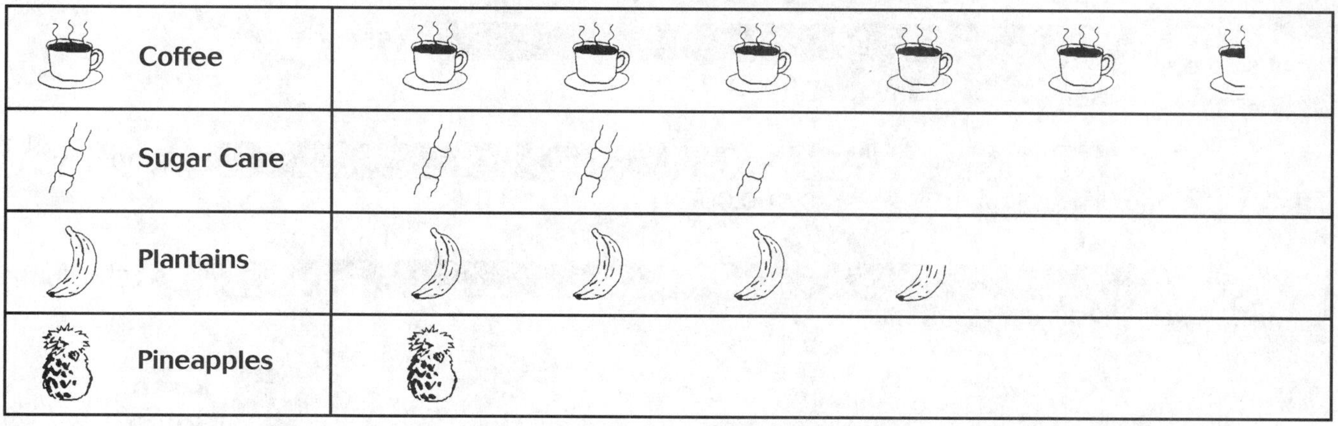

Each picture stands for $10 million dollars ($10,000,000) in sales each year.

Study the graph. Use the graph to answer the questions. Darken the circle by the best answer.

1. What kind of crop did Puerto Rico export the most?
Ⓐ coffee
Ⓑ sugar cane
Ⓒ plantains
Ⓓ pineapples

2. About how much more coffee was sold than sugar cane?
Ⓐ 2 times more
Ⓑ 5 times more
Ⓒ 6 times more
Ⓓ 10 times more

3. Plantains are a special kind of banana. About how much money did Puerto Rico earn from its plantain crop?
Ⓐ $3 million
Ⓑ $30 million
Ⓒ $35 million
Ⓓ $45 million

4. What would probably happen to Puerto Rico's economy if the coffee crop failed one year?
Ⓐ It would make much less money.
Ⓑ It would make the same amount of money.
Ⓒ It would make more money.
Ⓓ It would make no money at all.

Nonfiction Comprehension: Grades 5–6, SV 8948-6

Name _____ Date_____

North and South in the Civil War

At the time of the Civil War, the North had more miles of railroad track than the South. The double bar graph below compares the North and the South in other ways at the beginning of the Civil War.

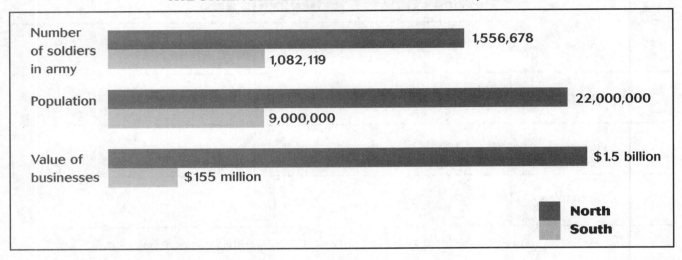

1. Which side in the war had the larger population?

_____

2. Which side had businesses that were more valuable?

_____

3. How many more soldiers were in the Union (North) Army than in the Confederate (South) Army?

_____

4. Which side do you think was stronger at the beginning of the Civil War? Use the information from the bar graphs to explain your answer.

_____

_____

_____

_____

_____

Name _____ Date _____

Population of the North and South in 1860

    A circle graph, also called a pie graph, is a circle that has been divided into sections that look like pieces of a pie. All the pie sections add up to 100 percent of the circle. *Percent* means parts of 100. The two circle graphs below give percents of the **population** of the North and the South in 1860. The two graphs can be compared.

COMPARING POPULATIONS

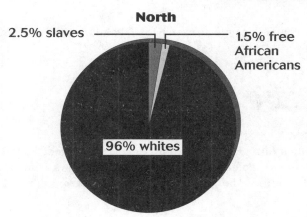

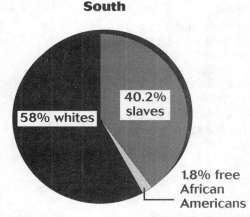

North

2.5% slaves — 1.5% free African Americans

96% whites

Total population: Almost 22,000,000

South

58% whites — 40.2% slaves

1.8% free African Americans

Total population: Almost 9,000,000

 **Study the two graphs. Use your knowledge about multiplying percents to choose the correct answer for each question from the right column.**

1. The North had more than _____ white people in 1860.

2. The slave population in the South was about _____.

3. The slave population in the North was about _____.

4. There were fewer than 200,000 free African Americans in the _____ in 1860.

a. 550,000

b. 21,000,000

c. North

d. 3,600,000

e. South

 **Write a complete sentence to answer the question.**

5. Compare the populations in the North and the South. How were they different?

_____

_____

_____

_____

_____

Lesson 2: Graphs
Nonfiction Comprehension: Grades 5–6, SV 8948-6

LESSON 3

Charts and Time Lines

Summary
"The Bill of Rights" (page 15): A chart explains the rights guaranteed in the first ten amendments to the U.S. Constitution.

"Circular Flow Model" (page 17): This article explains the economic meanings of producers and consumers and includes a circular flow chart illustrating the transfer of money in an economy.

"Time Line: 1925–1945" (page 18): The time line details some of the key historical events between 1925 and 1945.

Selection Type
Social Studies Articles

Comprehension Skill
Use Visual Aids for Information

Standards
Reading
• Use a variety of appropriate reference materials, including representations of information such as diagrams, maps, and charts, to gather information.

Social Studies
• Learn the basic ideas set forth in the Declaration of Independence, Constitution, and Bill of Rights.
• Describe how consumers and businesses interact in the United States economy.
• Put in chronological order important events in major study units.

VOCABULARY

Introduce the vocabulary words. Write the words on the board. Help students find a definition for each word. Have students use each word in a sentence.

"The Bill of Rights"
amendments   rights

"Circular Flow Model"
producers   consumers
interact

Tap Prior Knowledge
"The Bill of Rights": Ask the students to name some rights they have. Ask them where these rights come from.

"Circular Flow Model": Ask the students if they get an allowance. What do they do with their money? Do they know how money moves in an economy?

"Time Line: 1925–1945": Ask the students if they know any facts about the Great Depression or World War II. Did their grandparents live through these events?

Skill to Emphasize
Review the section about charts and time lines on page 5. Point out the charts and time line in the selections.

DURING READING

Preview Text Features
Point out the charts and their titles. The flowchart in "Circular Flow Model" shows the circular movement of money. Point out the directions of the arrows. Point out the time line in "Time Line: 1925–1945" and the sequential order of years. Boldfaced words indicate vocabulary words.

Comprehending the Selection
Ask the students: *What does the chart show?* or *What does the time line show?* Ask the students how the visual aid helps them to learn more about the topic.

AFTER READING

Reinforce the Comprehension Skill
Remind the students that charts and time lines organize information in an easy-to-understand format. Ask the students if they think charts and time lines are a good way to show information. Ask them what other kinds of charts they might have used that day.

Assess
Have the students complete the activities for each selection.

WRITE ABOUT IT

Have the students make a time line that shows their daily schedule. They should include about six daily activities and the times that they do each activity.

AT HOME

Have the students search through the newspaper or news magazines for charts or time lines and bring these visual aids to school to share with the class.

Name _____ Date_____

The Bill of Rights

The Bill of Rights contains the first ten **amendments** to the Constitution of the United States. The Bill of Rights guarantees basic **rights** to the people of this nation. The chart below tells what each amendment means.

Amendment 1:   **Basic freedoms**. Protects freedom of religion, freedom of speech, freedom of the press, freedom to hold meetings, and freedom to ask the government to correct problems. Keeps the government from creating an official religion.

Amendment 2:   **Right to bear arms**. Gives people the right to have guns, subject to laws of state and federal governments.

Amendment 3:   **Quartering of soldiers**. Protects people from having to give room and board to soldiers.

Amendment 4:   **Freedom from unlawful searches and arrests**. Keeps the police from being able to search and arrest people unlawfully.

Amendment 5:   **Rights of people accused of crimes**. Protects people accused of crimes from being taken to trial unfairly and being given unfair punishments.

Amendment 6:   **Trial by jury**. Gives people accused of crimes the right to a speedy public trial by jury. Spells out how the trial is to be conducted.

Amendment 7:   **Civil trials**. Gives people involved in noncriminal lawsuits the right to a jury trial.

Amendment 8:   **Bails, fines, and punishments**. Protects people from unfair bails, fines, and punishments.

Amendment 9:   **Rights to the people.** People have more than just those rights listed in the Constitution.

Amendment 10:   **Rights reserved for the states and the people**. All powers not given to the federal government belong to the states or the people themselves.

Nonfiction Comprehension: Grades 5–6, SV 8948-6

Name _____ Date_____

Comprehension Review

 Darken the circle by the best answer.

1. The first ten amendments to the ____ are contained in the Bill of Rights.
   Ⓐ Declaration of Independence
   Ⓑ Supreme Court
   Ⓒ Statue of Liberty
   Ⓓ Constitution

2. The Second Amendment gives people the right to bear arms. A synonym for *arms* is ____.
   Ⓐ soldiers
   Ⓑ guns
   Ⓒ religions
   Ⓓ trials

3. Freedom of speech is guaranteed in the ____.
   Ⓐ First Amendment
   Ⓑ Fourth Amendment
   Ⓒ Sixth Amendment
   Ⓓ Tenth Amendment

4. The Sixth Amendment guarantees ____.
   Ⓐ freedom of religion
   Ⓑ trial by jury
   Ⓒ freedom from unlawful searches
   Ⓓ the right to bear arms

5. All powers not given to the federal government or the states belong to ____.
   Ⓐ the police
   Ⓑ the President
   Ⓒ the people
   Ⓓ the army

6. The Third Amendment says that ____.
   Ⓐ soldiers cannot be quartered in your home
   Ⓑ the police cannot arrest people unlawfully
   Ⓒ people in lawsuits can have a jury trial
   Ⓓ people have the freedom to hold meetings

 Write a few sentences to answer the question.

7. Which amendment in the Bill of Rights do you think is the most important? Explain why.

_____

_____

Nonfiction Comprehension: Grades 5–6, SV 8948-6

Circular Flow Model

Producers are sellers. Producers are people or businesses that make goods or provide services. Producers sell their goods or services to consumers. **Consumers** are buyers. Consumers spend money to get the things they need or want.

Most businesses are both producers and consumers. Households work the same way. People buy goods and services from businesses. People also sell their own labor to the businesses. So, people are producers and consumers, too.

The circular flow model is about the transfer of goods and services. It shows how businesses and households **interact**. People in households sell their human resources to businesses. Then, they use the money they earn to buy goods and services from the businesses. Financial businesses, such as banks, direct the flow of money between businesses and households.

For example, Yvonne works at Babu's Store. She sells her labor to the store. For her labor, she is paid money. She then uses some of the money to buy her groceries at the store. Yvonne and Babu's Store interact.

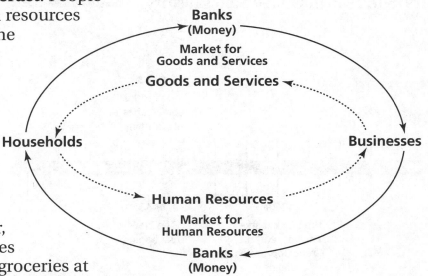

Darken the circle by the best answer.

1. ____ sell goods and services.
   Ⓐ Producers
   Ⓑ Consumers
   Ⓒ Circles
   Ⓓ Outputs

2. ____ buy goods and services.
   Ⓐ Producers
   Ⓑ Consumers
   Ⓒ Inputs
   Ⓓ Circles

3. The ____ shows the transfer of goods and services.
   Ⓐ financial business
   Ⓑ consumer
   Ⓒ circular flow model
   Ⓓ household

4. The circular flow model shows how businesses and households ____.
   Ⓐ change
   Ⓑ service
   Ⓒ entertain
   Ⓓ interact

Name _____ Date _____

Time Line: 1925–1945

A time line shows the order of events in a certain period of time. The events and time they happen are presented along a vertical or horizontal line. This line shows the sequence of events. The time line below shows important events from 1925 to 1945 in United States history.

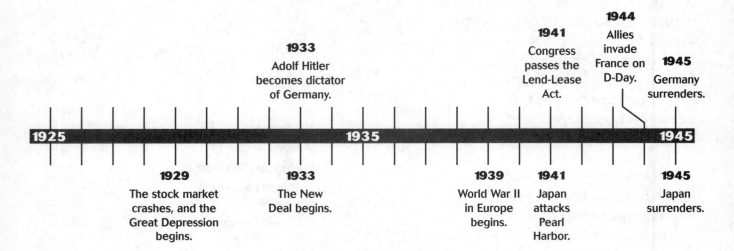

1933 Adolf Hitler becomes dictator of Germany.

1941 Congress passes the Lend-Lease Act.

1944 Allies invade France on D-Day.

1945 Germany surrenders.

1925 ———————————————— 1935 ———————————————— 1945

1929 The stock market crashes, and the Great Depression begins.

1933 The New Deal begins.

1939 World War II in Europe begins.

1941 Japan attacks Pearl Harbor.

1945 Japan surrenders.

➤ **Use the time line to answer the questions. Darken the circle by the best answer.**

1. The stock market crash in ____ was the start of the Great Depression.
   Ⓐ 1925
   Ⓑ 1929
   Ⓒ 1933
   Ⓓ 1944

2. In 1933, ____ became the dictator of Germany.
   Ⓐ New Deal
   Ⓑ Pearl Harbor
   Ⓒ Lend Lease
   Ⓓ Adolf Hitler

3. Japan attacked ____ on December 7, 1941.
   Ⓐ France
   Ⓑ Pearl Harbor
   Ⓒ the stock market
   Ⓓ Adolf Hitler

4. Thousands of Allied soldiers invaded France on ____ on June 6, 1944.
   Ⓐ Labor Day
   Ⓑ Valentine Day
   Ⓒ A-Day
   Ⓓ D-Day

LESSON 4

SELECTION DETAILS

Summary

"The Great Plains" (page 20): Maps can give many kinds of information. This map gives the geographical location of the Great Plains, along with details about climate and terrain.

"Reading a Resource Map" (page 21): A resource map tells the location of a natural resource. This map shows the different kinds of trees and forests in the United States.

Selection Type
Social Studies Articles

Comprehension Skill
Use Visual Aids for Information

Standards

Reading
• Use a variety of appropriate reference materials, including representations of information such as diagrams, maps, and charts, to gather information.

Social Studies
• Use maps to identify physical and human features of North America.
• Understand map keys showing economics and resources.

VOCABULARY

Introduce the vocabulary words. Write the words on the board. Help students find a definition for each word. Have students use each word in a sentence.

"Reading a Resource Map"
*population   resource
precipitation*

Tap Prior Knowledge

"The Great Plains": Ask the students if they have ever used a map to learn more about a place. Do they know where the Great Plains are?

"Reading a Resource Map": Ask the students if they have used any wood products lately. What kind of wood was it? Where do they think the wood came from?

Skill to Emphasize

Review the section about maps on page 5. Point out the maps in the selections.

Preview Text Features

Point out the title of the map in each article. Point out the compass rose on each map. Have the students name the four cardinal directions: north, south, east, and west. Point out the map key in the resource map and the different kinds of shading used to show the different kinds of trees. Boldfaced words indicate vocabulary word.

Comprehending the Selection

Ask the students: *What does the map show*? Ask the students how the map helps them to learn more about the place.

Reinforce the Comprehension Skill

Remind the students that a map gives information about a place. Ask the students if they think maps are a good way to show information. Ask them what other kinds of maps they might have used that day, such as a weather map.

Assess

Have the students complete the activities for each selection.

 **WRITE ABOUT IT**

Have the students do research on natural resources or crops grown in their state. They should gather information on at least three resources or crops. Then, have the students draw an outline map of their state; they should include a title and a map key that uses a symbol for each resource or crop. Finally, they should shade in the areas of the state in which those resources or crops are found.

AT HOME

Have the students search through the newspaper or news magazines for maps. Have them bring these maps to school to share with the class. Discuss what information the maps show.

The Great Plains

A region has places that may share similar climates, landforms, businesses, products, and culture. The Great Plains is a large region of flat plains and low hills stretching from western Texas to northern Canada and from the Mississippi River to the Rocky Mountains. The Great Plains has very hot summers and very cold winters. It has a dry climate with less than 20 inches of rain a year. Tornadoes, thunderstorms, and blizzards are common weather problems in this region.

Ten states make up the Great Plains region of the United States. These states are shaded on the map.

Use the paragraphs above and the map to answer the questions. Write complete sentences.

1. What are the names of five states in the Great Plains region?

   _____

2. What are the four major rivers that run through the Great Plains?

   _____

3. What are two physical features shared by places in this region?

   _____

4. What is the climate like in the Great Plains?

   _____

Nonfiction Comprehension: Grades 5–6, SV 8948-6

Name _____ Date_____

Reading a Resource Map

Some maps show only one kind of information. A **population** map shows how many people live in different areas. A **precipitation** map shows how much rain or rain and snow an area gets each year. The map below is a **resource** map. This map shows where different kinds of trees and forests grow in the United States.

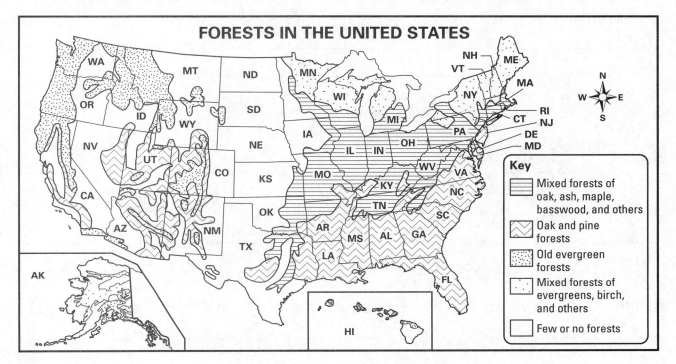

FORESTS IN THE UNITED STATES

Key
- Mixed forests of oak, ash, maple, basswood, and others
- Oak and pine forests
- Old evergreen forests
- Mixed forests of evergreens, birch, and others
- Few or no forests

 Darken the circle by the best answer.

1. The main trees in Ohio are ____.
   Ⓐ oak and pine
   Ⓑ old evergreen
   Ⓒ oak, ash, maple, and basswood
   Ⓓ old evergreen and birch

2. The main trees in Nebraska are ____.
   Ⓐ oak and pine
   Ⓑ old evergreen
   Ⓒ oak, ash, and maple
   Ⓓ None of the above

Nonfiction Comprehension: Grades 5–6, SV 8948-6

Comprehension Review

Name _____ **Date** _____

➡ Use the paragraph and the map on page 21 to answer the questions. Write complete sentences.

1. What are three states in which you would find old evergreen forests?

   _____

   _____

2. What kind of forest grows in the Northwest part of the United States?

   _____

   _____

3. What are the main trees in the Southeast part of the United States?

   _____

   _____

4. Find the state where you live. What kinds of trees or forests grow in your state?

   _____

   _____

5. Find the Great Plains on the map. What kind of trees can be found on the Great Plains? Why do you think that is? Explain.

   _____

   _____

   _____

   _____

   _____

   _____

   _____

   _____

Lesson 4: Maps
Nonfiction Comprehension: Grades 5–6, SV 8948-6

UNIT 2 — Main Idea and Details

Nonfiction articles, for the most part, deal with *facts*. Writing that gives only facts is called informative writing. The writer provides details about who, what, when, where, or how. The reader of factual writing must first be concerned with details, the facts of the article.

Sometimes the writer will also ask why and then answer this question by drawing conclusions based on the facts. This kind of writing is called interpretive writing. Sometimes the reader must interpret, too. The reader may have to identify the main idea.

• Main Idea (Lesson 5)

The main idea is the main point the writer is trying to make in the article. The main idea is not always stated directly in the article. How do readers decide what the main idea of an article is? First, they have to identify the topic of the article. The main idea will be some specific comment the writer is making about the topic. Usually, each paragraph has a main idea or topic sentence. Readers can put the topic sentences together to find the main idea of the article.

The main idea cannot be a statement not supported by the article. The main idea cannot be a statement that is only a detail.

To find the main idea of an article:
- Use the Main Idea Map on page 118.
- Read the article carefully.
- Find the topic of the article.
- Decide what all the sentences say about the topic.
- Ask yourself, "What is this article mostly about?"
- The title often gives a clue about the main idea.
- The main idea may be stated in the first paragraph.
- Write and revise the main idea.

Research Base
"Learning how to read informational texts involves strategies such as gathering information, summarizing and synthesizing information, and making connections to prior knowledge. Readers of informational texts must analyze where information is located within the overall organizational framework." (*Guiding Readers and Writers: Grades 3–6*, p. 400)

• Details (Lesson 6)

Details are facts that tell who, what, when, where, and how about a topic. Details add information to a story and make it more interesting. They should always support the main idea. To show their comprehension, readers are often asked to remember details from an article.

By reading carefully, readers can remember more details. By remembering more details, readers can more easily determine the main idea.

To recall specific facts and details:
- Use the Main Idea Map on page 118.
- Read the article carefully.
- Try to answer who, what, when, where, and how about the topic of the article.
- Read and think about the question carefully.
- Reread the article if necessary to answer the question.

• Summary (Lesson 7)

A summary is a short account of the main idea and key details of an article. A summary should include only the most important points in an article. Key details from the beginning, middle, and end of the article should be included. Readers must sometimes summarize an article when they need to condense the information in an article.

The ability to write a good summary shows the reader's comprehension of the article's main idea and key details.

To summarize an article:
- Use the Summary Chart on page 119.
- Read the article carefully, then put it aside.
- Think about the main idea and important details.
- Write the summary without looking at the article.
- Include only the main idea and important details.
- Do include the author's name (if given) and the title of the article.
- Do not use sentences, phrases, or direct quotes from the article.
- Do not use minor details, explanations, or examples.

• Graphic Organizers

Main Idea Map   page 118
Summary Chart   page 119

Nonfiction Comprehension: Grades 5–6, SV 8948-6

Main Idea

Summary

"Find the Main Idea" (sample paragraphs, page 25): The sample paragraphs give practice in identifying the main idea in short selections.

"The Wonders of Caves" (page 27): This article discusses the features of caves and the sport of spelunking.

Selection Type

Social Studies Article

Comprehension Skill

Identify Main Idea

Standards

Reading
• Identify main idea and details.

Social Studies
• Explain how physical processes produce distinctive landforms and natural structures.

VOCABULARY

Introduce the vocabulary words for "The Wonders of Caves." Write the words on the board. Help students find a definition for each word. Have students use each word in a sentence.

spelunking   chambers
stalactites   stalagmites
reliable   descent
enthusiastic   unique
spectacular   fragile

BEFORE READING

Tap Prior Knowledge

Ask the students if they have ever been in a cave. What was it like? Was the cave lighted? Ask them what they think it would be like to explore a cave without lighting or pathways.

Skill to Emphasize

Review the section about main idea on page 23. Tell the students that they will try to find what each selection is mostly about. Have the students do the practice paragraphs before they move on to the "The Wonders of Caves" reading selection.

DURING READING

Preview Text Features

Each paragraph has a topic sentence. Point out the topic sentence in each paragraph. Tell the students that if they think about all the topic sentences, they should be able to determine the main idea of the selection more easily. Subtitles tell what is in each section of the article. Illustrations help present concepts such as knots, stalactites, and stalagmites. Boldfaced words indicate vocabulary words.

Comprehending the Selection

Model how to identify the main idea by asking: *What is this story mostly about?*

AFTER READING

Reinforce the Comprehension Skill

Tell the students that the title of the selection often includes the topic, as in this article about caves. The main idea is some point about the topic. What is the author saying about caves? (that caves are wonderful and the exploration of them is a fun activity)

Distribute copies of the Main Idea Map on page 118. Have the students complete the map for the "The Wonders of Caves" article.

Assess

Have the students complete the activities for each selection.

WRITE ABOUT IT

Have the students write a paragraph about an exploration they have made. What equipment did they need? What safety guidelines did they use?

AT HOME

Have the students look for articles about caves in newspapers or news magazines. Have them bring these articles to school to share with the class.

Name _____   Date_____

Find the Main Idea

➡ Read each paragraph. Identify what it is mainly about. Darken the circle by the best answer.

The mongoose is a small meat-eating mammal. It eats snakes and is quick enough to avoid the snake if it strikes. Its speed enables it to kill the king cobra, one of the most poisonous snakes. The mongoose is one of the world's most active animals. With its quickness, it is also a successful hunter of rats, mice, and wild birds.

1. This paragraph is mainly about the ____.
   Ⓐ world's most poisonous snake
   Ⓑ slow and lazy mongoose
   Ⓒ hunting skills of the mongoose
   Ⓓ story "Rikki-tikki-tavi"

The whale is often mistaken for a fish instead of a mammal. The whale breathes air, has hair on parts of its body, and is warm-blooded. Baby whales, called calves, get milk from their mother's body. These are all characteristics of mammals.

2. This paragraph is mainly about ____.
   Ⓐ baby whales called calves
   Ⓑ whales being mammals
   Ⓒ habits of the blue whale
   Ⓓ the whale's blood

The paper wasp and the white-faced hornet build their nests out of paper. The yellow jacket, another kind of wasp, builds big nests in the ground. The potter wasp builds little jug-like nests on twigs, and the mud dauber builds a mud nest with many rooms. The cuckoo wasp doesn't build a nest. It lays eggs in the mud dauber's nest when the mud dauber is away.

3. This paragraph is mainly about the ____.
   Ⓐ lazy, tricky cuckoo wasp
   Ⓑ many kinds of wasp nests
   Ⓒ asps living in colonies
   Ⓓ white-faced hornet

Some breeds of sheep raised in the United States are the Merino, Hampshire, and Cheviot. The Karakul, also called a fat-tail sheep, is found in Asia. Wild sheep are found in Asia, northern Africa, and southern Europe. The bighorn, found in the Rocky Mountains, is another wild breed.

4. This story is mainly about ____.
   Ⓐ various breeds of sheep
   Ⓑ raising sheep for wool
   Ⓒ sheep in the United States
   Ⓓ having no more wild sheep

Nonfiction Comprehension: Grades 5–6, SV 8948-6

Name _____ Date _____

Read each paragraph. Identify what it is mainly about. Darken the circle by the best answer. Then write a complete sentence to answer each question.

Stephen Foster composed songs, such as "My Old Kentucky Home," that we still sing today. Even though he was a talented writer of songs, he had a very unhappy life. He died at the age of 38, homeless, without friends, and almost penniless. In fact, he made very little money from any of the 200 songs he wrote.

5. The story is mainly about the _____.
   Ⓐ unhappy life of Stephen Foster
   Ⓑ 100 songs by Stephen Foster
   Ⓒ way a composer gets ideas
   Ⓓ death of Stephen Foster at 38

6. How did you know? _____

_____

Many people collect seashells. Shells have been used for money by various people of the world. Some shells are used for decoration. Some animals are fed ground-up shells, and sometimes ground shells are added to soil to improve its quality.

7. This story is mainly about _____.
   Ⓐ using shells for game markers
   Ⓑ the many uses of seashells
   Ⓒ feeding animals ground shells
   Ⓓ how shells can ruin soil quality

8. How did you know? _____

_____

The great Mississippi River divides the 48-state part of the United States into two parts. It runs from near Canada to the Gulf of Mexico. It is more than a mile wide in some places. Many large and important rivers flow into it. A huge amount of water flows down the Mississippi.

9. What is the main idea of this paragraph?

_____

_____

The Wonders of Caves

Have you ever used a flashlight to explore a dark, mysterious place? Have you ever seen pictures of famous caves such as Carlsbad Caverns? You can take a journey into these underground worlds. **Spelunking**, the hobby of exploring caves, is your ticket. With the right equipment and a careful leader, you can travel deep into the Earth. Fantastic underground spaces appear. Amazing rock shapes will surround you. You may see unusual creatures. You can find out how different caves formed. You can also learn how to protect them. But spelunking isn't for everyone. Read on to find out if spelunking is for you.

Caves and How They Form

Before you start spelunking, you need to know some facts about caves. Caves form when something hollows out spaces in rocks or ice. It can be water traveling underground or ocean waves pounding on cliffs. It can also be lava from volcanoes.

The caves that spelunkers often explore are limestone caves. These caves form in soft, limestone rock. As water seeps into the cracks, it wears away at the limestone. Slowly, over tens of thousands of years, the cracks get larger. More water flows in, and the process continues. When the water drains out, a cave is left behind.

A cave can have a single room or miles of tunnels and **chambers**. Incredible rock shapes can fill these underground spaces. Again, water is the cause. Water drips into underground spaces and interacts with the rock. Minerals enter the water. Then the water flows on, leaving some of these minerals behind.

The minerals form crystals that collect on the roofs and floors of caves. **Stalactites** hang from the roof of a cave like icicles. **Stalagmites** grow from the floor of a cave like columns. These and other rock formations are often white. Some reflect the colors of the minerals that helped form them.

Nonfiction Comprehension: Grades 5–6, SV 8948-6

Name _____ **Date**_____

Time to Go Spelunking!

Now that you know where you're going, you're ready to go spelunking. Wise spelunkers explore in groups. The last place you want to be stranded alone is in a cave! Trained guides can help.

Spelunkers also need **reliable** equipment. The **descent** into a cave is like mountain climbing in the opposite direction. Basic spelunking equipment is similar to what mountain climbers use. Strong ropes make climbing possible, and special tools attach ropes to cave walls. Special footwear makes it easier to explore hard-to-reach places. A hard hat protects you from falling rocks above. Caves are extremely dark. Spelunkers carry at least three light sources. One light source attaches to a spelunker's helmet so it is with him or her at all times. Caves can be cold, so most spelunkers wear heavy clothing for warmth.

Spelunkers tie their ropes with different kinds of knots. From the *farmer's hitch knot* to the *alpine butterfly knot*, spelunkers choose knots for different purposes. Some knots work well to hold people as they climb. Other knots are best for tying ropes together.

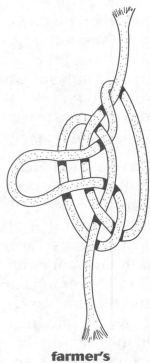

farmer's hitch knot

alpine butterfly knot

Name _____ Date_____

What's in a Cave?

Some caves contain bubbling streams. Others are filled with huge lakes. Spelunkers may use boats to travel through these caves. **Enthusiastic** spelunkers may take special training in diving. This lets them explore beneath the water's surface. Divers may even see fish swimming in these underground lakes!

Caving can open the door to many treasures. For example, people once made their homes in caves. Some have left stories behind in paintings, tools, and bones. Many **unique** animals also live in caves. These are creatures that prefer cold air and darkness. Keep on the lookout for bats, lizards, crickets, spiders, and more.

Caving offers plenty of excitement and a challenge. It also presents serious dangers. Most of all, it requires responsibility. Rock shapes can be **spectacular**, but they are often **fragile**. People can also threaten rare cave animals. Remember to leave caves as you found them. Don't take anything from a cave. And be sure to take your litter with you.

Now that you know what to do, pack up your caving gear. You are ready to try spelunking!

Some animals, such as bats and spiders, make their homes in caves.

Comprehension Review

 Darken the circle by the best answer.

1. Which of the following do you need when you go caving?
   Ⓐ an oxygen tank for breathing
   Ⓑ bags for collecting cave materials
   Ⓒ good lights and strong rope
   Ⓓ shorts and a light shirt

2. Limestone caves are formed when ____.
   Ⓐ water wears away soft rock
   Ⓑ construction leaves holes behind
   Ⓒ earthquakes shake up rocks
   Ⓓ underground gas explodes

3. Which of the following is a reason caving might be dangerous?
   Ⓐ Huge and scary animals live in caves.
   Ⓑ Cave minerals can be poisonous.
   Ⓒ Robbers often hide out in caves.
   Ⓓ It would be hard to reach a person that is lost or hurt.

4. Why do you think the author wrote this article?
   Ⓐ to tell a story about a favorite caving trip
   Ⓑ to tell readers about caving
   Ⓒ to get readers to believe that caving shouldn't be allowed
   Ⓓ to list cave animals that must be protected

 Answer the questions below in complete sentences.

5. Why do you think it would be important for a spelunker to tie a knot correctly?

_____

_____

6. What is one way that cave animals are unusual?

_____

_____

Lesson 5: Main Idea
Nonfiction Comprehension: Grades 5–6, SV 8948-6

Vocabulary Review

 Darken the circle by the best meaning for each underlined word.

1. This cave is full of tunnels and <u>chambers</u> to explore.
   Ⓐ holes
   Ⓑ large rooms
   Ⓒ long ropes
   Ⓓ a kind of stalagmite

2. Make your <u>descent</u> by placing each foot lower on the ladder.
   Ⓐ upward climb
   Ⓑ sideways climb
   Ⓒ lunch
   Ⓓ downward climb

3. Caves may contain <u>unique</u> life forms not seen anywhere else.
   Ⓐ very common
   Ⓑ dangerous
   Ⓒ one of a kind
   Ⓓ scary

4. Prepare to see <u>spectacular</u> rock shapes the next time you go caving.
   Ⓐ very tiny
   Ⓑ ordinary
   Ⓒ striped
   Ⓓ amazing

5. Spelunkers are <u>enthusiastic</u> about caving.
   Ⓐ excited
   Ⓑ nervous
   Ⓒ uninformed
   Ⓓ frightened

6. It is important to use <u>reliable</u> equipment when you go caving.
   Ⓐ cheap
   Ⓑ dependable
   Ⓒ interesting
   Ⓓ strange

Build Your Vocabulary

Dictionaries give word spellings to help you with pronunciations. They also give definitions.

 Write the correct word from the box. Then write the word's meaning.

> spelunking   stalagmites   stalactites

7. (stuh LAK tyts) _____

   _____

8. (spee LUNG king) _____

   _____

9. (stuh LAG myts) _____

   _____

Name _____ Date_____

Main Idea Chart

The main idea is the most important of an article. Writers use supporting details to tell more about the main idea. A paragraph may also have its own main idea and supporting details.

 Use the information from the article to fill in the main idea chart.

> **MAIN IDEA**
>
> Spelunking allows people to see the many wonders of caves.

SUPPORTING DETAIL	SUPPORTING DETAIL	SUPPORTING DETAIL
_____	_____	_____
_____	_____	_____
_____	_____	_____
_____	_____	_____
_____	_____	_____

Use the article to write answers in complete sentences.

1. Choose one paragraph in the article. Identify the paragraph and write the main idea in your own words.

_____

_____

_____

2. Write two supporting details for the main idea you chose.

_____

_____

_____

_____

_____

Nonfiction Comprehension: Grades 5–6, SV 8948-6

LESSON 6

BEFORE READING

Tap Prior Knowledge

"*Lusitania* Sunk by a Submarine": Ask the students if they ever read the newspaper. What kinds of articles do they read? What famous ships do they know about that have sunk? Have they ever heard of the *Lusitania*?

Skill to Emphasize

Review the section about details on page 23. Tell the students that they must pay attention to all the facts in the articles they read. Those facts are called details.

DURING READING

Preview Text Features

Each paragraph has a topic sentence. Point out the topic sentence in each paragraph. Each topic sentence is supported by detail sentences. The detail sentences give facts, or details, about the topic sentence. The subtitles also give details about the event. Boldfaced words indicate vocabulary words.

Comprehending the Selection

Model how to identify the details by asking: *What facts does the article tell about who, what, when, where, and how?*

AFTER READING

Reinforce the Comprehension Skill

Tell the students that the main idea is the general point the author is making. In this newspaper article, the main idea is contained in the title. The details are specific facts that help the author to achieve the main idea. Ask the students to identify some of the details in the article.

Distribute copies of the Main Idea Map on page 118. Have the students complete the map for the "*Lusitania* Sunk by a Submarine" article.

Assess

Have the students complete the activities for each selection.

WRITE ABOUT IT

Have the students write a story about how they might feel if they were on board the *Lusitania* when it was attacked.

AT HOME

Have the students search through the newspaper for an article about current events. Have the students list the important details of who, what, when, where, and how. Have the students bring their articles and lists to share with the class.

SELECTION DETAILS

Summary

"Find the Details" (sample paragraphs, page 34): The sample paragraphs give practice in identifying the details in short selections.

"*Lusitania* Sunk by a Submarine" (page 36): This newspaper article from 1915 gives details about the sinking of the ocean liner *Lusitania* by a German submarine.

Selection Type

Historical Newspaper Article

Comprehension Skill

Identify Details

Standards

Reading
• Identify main idea and supporting details.

Social Studies
• Identify primary and secondary sources historians use to understand the past, such as letters, diaries, and newspaper articles.

VOCABULARY

Introduce the vocabulary words for "*Lusitania* Sunk by a Submarine." Write the words on the board. Help students find a definition for each word. Have students use each word in a sentence.

elude	*stricken*
fatal	*steward*
non-combatants	*neutral*
dispatch	

Find the Details

→ **Read each paragraph. Darken the circle by the best answer.**

Asteroids travel in a path around the Sun just as planets do. They are not nearly as large as a planet, but one, named Vesta, is bright enough to be seen without a telescope. The largest known asteroid is Ceres. It is less than 500 miles across. More than 1,600 asteroids have been discovered, and new ones are being found all the time.

1. What is the largest known asteroid?
   Ⓐ Jupiter   Ⓒ the Sun
   Ⓑ Vesta   Ⓓ Ceres

Franklin D. Roosevelt, the 32nd President of the United States, is the only person who has held that office for more than two terms. When he was first elected, the country was in bad shape. Businesses were failing, and banks were closing their doors. He enacted some programs that gave people hope and was easily elected for a second term. By the time his second term was finished, the United States was involved in World War II. The people did not want to change Presidents in the middle of the war, so Roosevelt was elected to a third and fourth term. He died before his fourth term was finished and didn't see the end of the war.

2. Why was Roosevelt elected to his second term?
   Ⓐ It was the middle of the war.
   Ⓑ His programs gave people hope.
   Ⓒ Businesses were failing.
   Ⓓ He didn't see the end of the war.

Rodents are gnawing animals, such as rats, mice, chipmunks, beavers, and porcupines. They are mammals that live underground and above ground, in swamps and deserts, and in warm and cold areas. Their teeth never stop growing, so the constant gnawing doesn't wear them away. Most rodents eat plants, and some, like the field mouse, do a lot of damage to crops. Mice and rats are usually unwelcome visitors in our homes. The mouse is a pest, but the rat can carry dangerous diseases.

3. Why doesn't the gnawing wear away the teeth of a rodent?
   Ⓐ Rodents live underground.
   Ⓑ The teeth never stop growing.
   Ⓒ Rodents usually eat plants.
   Ⓓ Mice and rats visit our homes.

Nonfiction Comprehension: Grades 5–6, SV 8948-6

Name _____ Date _____

 Read the paragraph. Darken the circle by the best answer.

Thomas Alva Edison was a remarkable man and probably the world's greatest inventor. He was known as the "Wizard of Menlo Park" because of the amazing, almost magical things he created in Menlo Park, New Jersey. His most famous invention is the electric light, but he also invented the phonograph and motion pictures. Even though he made many improvements on the telegraph, he did not invent it. His sleeping habits were unusual. When working on a project in the lab, he would nap when sleepy and work upon waking, regardless of the time of day.

4. What was Thomas Edison's most famous invention?
    Ⓐ electric light   Ⓒ phonograph
    Ⓑ telegraph   Ⓓ motion pictures

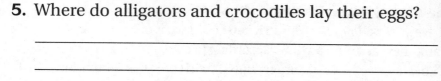 **Read the paragraph. Write complete sentences to answer the questions.**

Among the largest of the reptiles living today are the alligators and crocodiles. Some crocodiles grow to a length of over 20 feet. Like all reptiles, alligators and crocodiles are cold-blooded and must live in warm climates. They are meat-eaters, eating fish or small animals. They cannot breathe underwater, and they lay their eggs on land. Although alligators and crocodiles are similar in looks, their heads are shaped differently, and the crocodile has a lower tooth on both sides that shows when its jaws are shut.

5. Where do alligators and crocodiles lay their eggs?

_____

_____

_____

6. What do alligators and crocodiles eat?

_____

_____

7. How can you tell an alligator from a crocodile?

_____

_____

_____

    Nonfiction Comprehension: Grades 5–6, SV 8948-6

Name _____ Date_____

Lusitania Sunk by a Submarine

On Friday, May 7, 1915, a German submarine torpedoed a British passenger ship, the *Lusitania*. The ship, owned by the Cunard Company, sank near Ireland. This news article was in *The New York Times* the next day. Americans were shocked that Germany had attacked a ship that had so many passengers. On that day no one knew all the details about the disaster. Later people learned that 1,198 people had died, and 128 of those people were Americans.

LUSITANIA SUNK BY A SUBMARINE!

LONDON, Saturday, May 8—The Cunard liner *Lusitania*, which sailed out of New York last Saturday with 1,918 souls aboard, lies at the bottom of the ocean off the Irish coast.

She was sunk by a German submarine, which sent two torpedoes, crashing into her side, while the passengers, seemingly confident that the great, swift vessel could **elude** the German underwater craft, were having luncheon.

How many of the *Lusitania* passengers and crew were rescued cannot be told at present....Probably at least 1,000 persons, including many Americans, have lost their lives.

Sank in Fifteen Minutes.

The **stricken** vessel went down in less than half an hour, according to all reports. The most definite statement puts fifteen minutes as the time that passed between the **fatal** blow and the disappearance of the *Lusitania* beneath the waves.

There were 1,253 passengers from New York on board the steamship, including 200 who were transferred to her from the steamer *Cameronia*. The crew numbered 665. No names of the rescued are yet available.

(Story continued on page 37.)

Nonfiction Comprehension: Grades 5–6, SV 8948-6

Story of the Attack.

...Describing the experience of the *Lusitania*, the **steward** said:

"The passengers were at lunch when a submarine came up and fired two torpedoes, which struck the *Lusitania* on the starboard side, one forward and another in the engine room. They caused terrific explosions.

"Captain Turner immediately ordered the boats out....Ten boats were put into the water, and between 400 and 500 passengers entered them. The boat in which I was, approached the land with three other boats, and we were picked up shortly after 4 o'clock....

"I fear that few of the officers were saved. They acted bravely...."

Hit 10 Miles Off Kinsale Head.

This greatest sea tragedy of the war, because of the terrible loss of lives of **non-combatants** and citizens of **neutral** nations, took place about ten miles off the Old Head of Kinsale about 2 o'clock in the afternoon.

A **dispatch** to the Exchange Telegraph from Liverpool quotes the Cunard Company as stating that "the *Lusitania* was sunk without warning...."

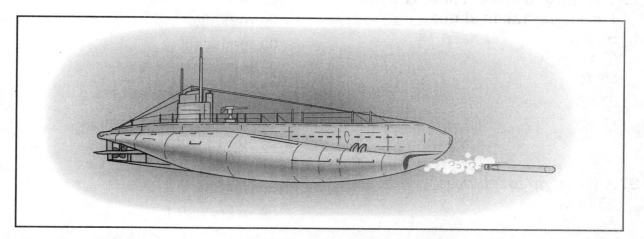

 Write complete sentences to answer the questions.

1. How did the German submarine sink the *Lusitania*?

   _____

2. How long did it take for the ship to sink?

   _____

3. What were passengers doing when the ship was attacked?

   _____

4. Where was the *Lusitania* when it sank?

   _____

Name _____ Date_____

Comprehension and Vocabulary Review

→ **Darken the circle by the best answer.**

1. The *Lusitania* was struck on the ____ side by two torpedoes.
- Ⓐ top
- Ⓑ port
- Ⓒ starboard
- Ⓓ back

2. The most definite report said the *Lusitania* sank in about ____ minutes.
- Ⓐ 2
- Ⓑ 15
- Ⓒ 45
- Ⓓ 60

3. A synonym for *elude* is ____.
- Ⓐ bake
- Ⓑ sink
- Ⓒ avoid
- Ⓓ go before

4. A steward is a ____.
- Ⓐ captain
- Ⓑ waiter
- Ⓒ singer
- Ⓓ submariner

5. A non-combatant is ____.
- Ⓐ a kind of torpedo
- Ⓑ a German submarine
- Ⓒ a lifeboat
- Ⓓ a person who is not a soldier

6. Another word for *dispatch* is ____.
- Ⓐ flat tire
- Ⓑ message
- Ⓒ life jacket
- Ⓓ luncheon

7. Something that is fatal is ____.
- Ⓐ not harmful
- Ⓑ friendly
- Ⓒ deadly
- Ⓓ overweight

8. A neutral nation in World War I was one that ____.
- Ⓐ helped the Germans
- Ⓑ was not involved in the fighting
- Ⓒ did not have torpedoes
- Ⓓ sank passenger ships

LESSON 7

Summary

SELECTION DETAILS

Summary
"Summarizing Practice" (sample paragraphs, page 40): The sample paragraphs give practice in summarizing the main idea and details in short selections.

"Sojourner Truth" (page 41): This article gives a brief account of the life of this famous woman.

Selection Type
Social Studies Article

Comprehension Skill
Summarize Information

Standards
Reading
• Summarize the main information in a nonfiction text.

Social Studies
• Explain the course and consequences of the Civil War, with emphasis on contributions of key individuals and the role of African Americans.

VOCABULARY

Introduce the vocabulary words for "Sojourner Truth." Write the words on the board. Help students find a definition for each word. Have students use each word in a sentence.

outlawed   injustice
sojourner   labored

 **BEFORE READING**

Tap Prior Knowledge
"Sojourner Truth": Ask the students what they think the life of a slave might have been like. How do they think a slave might have felt when he or she gained freedom? What contributions can they make now to help other people?

Skill to Emphasize
Review the section about summary on page 23. Tell the students that a summary leaves out unimportant ideas and details. A good summary is short and to the point. The title and subtitles in an article can help students to write a good summary.

 **DURING READING**

Preview Text Features
Preview the article with students. Have the students pay attention to the title and details in the article. These details will help them arrive at a main idea and write a better summary. Point out the illustration. Boldfaced words indicate vocabulary words.

Comprehending the Selection
Model how to summarize the article by asking: *What are the important ideas and details in this article?*

 **AFTER READING**

Reinforce the Comprehension Skill
Tell the students that a good summary is short, and it includes only the most important ideas in the article. Have the students summarize the "Sojourner Truth" article. Distribute copies of the Summary Chart on page 119. Have the students complete the chart for the article to help them write the summary.

Assess
Have the students complete the activities for each selection.

 **WRITE ABOUT IT**

Have the students write about how they might feel if they were a slave. Would they try to escape? How would they do it?

AT HOME

Have the students search through the newspaper or news magazines for articles about people who use their lives to help others. Have the students summarize the articles. Then have the students bring their articles and summaries to share with the class.

Summarizing Practice

A summary is a short account of the main idea and key details of an article. A summary should include only the most important points in an article. Summaries are good for condensing the information in an article.

Darken the circle by the best answer for each question.

The haddock is an ocean fish and one of the most important fish along the east coast of the United States. It is caught along the New England coast, Newfoundland, and Canada. It weighs from three to fifteen pounds and can be eaten fresh, dried, or smoked.

1. Which of the following is the best summary of the paragraph above?
   Ⓐ A haddock can range in size and is found along the east coast of the United States.
   Ⓑ The haddock, found along the east coast, is an important fish that is used for food.
   Ⓒ Haddock can be prepared in a number of ways.
   Ⓓ The haddock is a kind of fish along the east coast.

Cellulose is the woody part of plants that gives them stiffness. Without cellulose, people would be without thousands of articles they use every day. Cotton fibers, linen cloth, coco matting, and manila rope are largely cellulose. Wood, too, is mostly cellulose, as is the paper that is made from wood. Cellulose is also used in the manufacture of certain plastics.

2. Which of the following is the best summary of the above story?
   Ⓐ Cellulose, the woody part of plants, gives us many products.
   Ⓑ Cellulose is used in the manufacture of plastic products.
   Ⓒ Plants are stiff because of cellulose.
   Ⓓ Linen cloth is the product of plant cellulose.

Dinosaurs once roamed the world. We know about the different kinds of these animals from bones we have found and footprints left in stone. Some dinosaurs were the size of roosters, and others were as large as houses. Some ate meat, and others were plant-eaters. Some of them were like birds, and others were like lizards.

3. Which of the following is the best summary of the above story?
   Ⓐ Some dinosaurs were like birds, and others were more like lizards.
   Ⓑ Dinosaurs lived all over the world.
   Ⓒ All dinosaurs were large.
   Ⓓ Dinosaurs came in different sizes, ate different foods, and looked different.

Nonfiction Comprehension: Grades 5–6, SV 8948-6

Sojourner Truth

When Abraham Lincoln was elected President in 1860, Sojourner Truth was an old woman. She had been born a slave in 1797. Her real name was Isabella. She lived on a farm in New York State.

Sojourner was bought and sold several times. She married and had five children, all slaves. It made her sad and angry when two of her daughters were sold away from her. Finally, she ran away. A year later, in 1828, slavery was **outlawed** in New York. She went to New York City and worked as a servant.

But Sojourner wanted more. She wanted to speak out against **injustice**. She wanted to travel and spread God's word. She called herself Sojourner Truth. A **sojourner** is a traveler. Sojourner set off on her travels with only 25 cents. She traveled all over the country. Sojourner became a well-known speaker. She spoke against slavery. She spoke for the rights of women. At that time, neither women nor African Americans could vote or own property.

Once, at a big meeting, Sojourner heard a man say that women weren't equal to men. Sojourner stood up and answered him. "I have **labored**, I have planted and harvested crops. And aren't I a woman?" This speech made her famous.

Sojourner also helped escaped slaves find homes and jobs in the North. She did what she could do to help African Americans have a better life.

She was invited to the White House by President Lincoln. When Sojourner died, she was 86 years old. Her death made many people very sad. Sojourner Truth was the most famous African American woman of her time.

Name _____ Date_____

Comprehension and Vocabulary Review

 Darken the circle by the best answer.

1. Slavery was outlawed in New York in
   ____.
   Ⓐ 1797
   Ⓑ 1828
   Ⓒ 1860
   Ⓓ 1886

2. After slavery was outlawed in New
   York, Sojourner became a ____ in
   New York City.
   Ⓐ slave
   Ⓑ President
   Ⓒ servant
   Ⓓ farmer

3. This article is mainly about ____.
   Ⓐ how hard the lives of slaves were
   Ⓑ President Abraham Lincoln
   Ⓒ Sojourner Truth's real name
   Ⓓ how Sojourner Truth worked to
      make life better for others

4. When it was outlawed in New York,
   slavery ____ there.
   Ⓐ was made illegal
   Ⓑ was made legal
   Ⓒ became very popular
   Ⓓ did not end

5. You can conclude from the article
   that ____.
   Ⓐ President Lincoln did not live in
      the White House
   Ⓑ everyone could vote in
      Sojourner's time
   Ⓒ Sojourner liked to be a slave
   Ⓓ Sojourner thought that all people
      were equal

6. Sojourner began her travels with
   only ____.
   Ⓐ a tent and some hiking boots
   Ⓑ an old bicycle
   Ⓒ a mule and a sack of corn
   Ⓓ 25 cents

7. A synonym for *labored* is ____.
   Ⓐ played
   Ⓑ worked
   Ⓒ shopped
   Ⓓ spoke loudly

8. *Injustice* means ____.
   Ⓐ inside a courtroom
   Ⓑ things that are equal for all
   Ⓒ an act that is wrong or unfair
   Ⓓ made of old metal

Name _____ Date_____

Summarize the Article

When you summarize an article, you tell the main idea and the key details. Finding the most important ideas in each paragraph can help you to write a summary.

➡ Use the article about Sojourner Truth on page 41 to complete the summary chart.

Important Idea in Paragraph 1: _____

_____

Important Idea in Paragraph 2: _____

_____

Important Idea in Paragraph 3: _____

_____

Important Idea in Paragraph 4: _____

_____

Important Idea in Paragraph 5: _____

_____

Important Idea in Paragraph 6: _____

_____

Summary:

_____

_____

_____

_____

_____

_____

_____

    Nonfiction Comprehension: Grades 5–6, SV 8948-6

UNIT 3 Narration

Narration is concerned with the sequence of events or details in time. Sometimes this sequence is presented as a plot, as in a short story or historical narrative. Sometimes the sequence is a list, as in a how-to project. The sequence usually goes from beginning to end in chronological order, just as we move through time. Many times, a strong relationship exists between events. One event may cause another event. This relationship is called cause and effect.

Sequence

Sequence is the order of events in a narrative or process. Students should be able to retell the order of events in a narration. Some words serve as signals to show the order of events. Such words as *first*, *next*, *then*, and *finally* may also be used in a selection to show alphabetical or numerical order.

To find the sequence of an event or process:
- Use the Sequence Chart on page 120.
- Read the article carefully.
- Look for signal words or numbers that show the order of events.
- Think about the sequence, or order of events.
- Decide in what order events occurred.
- Retell or write a brief list of the events in order.

Narration of Event (Lesson 8)

Narration of event is a form that should be familiar to students. They tell stories of what they did. They read stories of fictional characters. Biographies and historical occurrences contain narration of events. A biography tells the events in a person's life. A historical occurrence contains a narration of events, such as the sequence of events in World War II.

A narration of event usually includes a sense of beginning, middle, and end. It should have a setting and at least one person or historical character. A problem is usually introduced, and some outcome to the problem is indicated. The narration of event may include some emotional impact and may include an insight or point about human nature or behavior.

To recall the sequence in a narration of event:
- Use the Sequence Chart on page 120.
- Read the title for information about the event or person.
- Read the article carefully.
- Look for signal words that show the order of events.
- Decide in what order the events occurred.
- Divide the event into beginning, middle, and end.
- Retell or write a brief list of the events in order.

Narration of Process (Lesson 9)

Narration of process is another form that should be familiar to students. One kind of process is the how-to. A how-to can be instructional, such as how to bake a cake, or it can be informational, such as how glass is made. Some processes can be quite complicated, such as the annual migratory cycle of some animals.

A narration of process includes a series of steps that also presents a sense of beginning, middle, and end. The end should indicate the completion of the process. The process essay may also include a list of materials needed, a cautionary list of things to do and not to do, and any tips or shortcuts that will facilitate the process.

To recall the sequence in a narration of process:
- Use the Sequence Chart on page 120.
- Read the title for information about the process.
- Read the article carefully.
- Look for signal words or numbers that show the order of steps.
- Note what the end result should be.
- Retell or write a brief list of the steps in order.

Cause and Effect (Lesson 10)

An article can tell about things that happen and why they happen. Why something happens is a cause. What happens because of it is an effect. In other words, a cause tells why an effect happens. Some words are used to signal causes and effects. The words *because* and *since* often introduce a cause. The words *therefore*, *so*, *thus*, and *as a result* often introduce an effect.

To identify causes and effects:
- Use the Cause-Effect Chart on page 121.
- Read the title for information about a cause or effect.
- Read the article carefully.
- Look for signal words that introduce a cause or effect.
- Decide which part of a sentence or paragraph is the cause and which part is the effect.
- Use that information to help answer *Why*?

Graphic Organizers

Sequence Chart	page 120
Cause-Effect Chart	page 121

Nonfiction Comprehension: Grades 5–6, SV 8948-6

Narration of Event

SELECTION DETAILS

Summary
"Find the Sequence" (page 46): The sample paragraphs give practice in identifying the sequence in short selections.

"Elizabeth Blackwell (1821–1910)" (page 47): This article recounts the life and efforts of the first woman doctor in the United States.

"A Night to Remember" (page 49): This article tells the events of the sinking of the *Titanic* in 1912.

Selection Type
Social Studies Articles

Comprehension Skill
Identify Sequence of Events in a Narration of Event

Standards
Reading
- Identify the order of events in a reading selection.
- Distinguish fact from fiction in a reading selection.

History
- Describe how social roles have both changed and endured in U.S. history.
- Put in chronological order important people and events.

VOCABULARY

Introduce the vocabulary words for each article. Write the words on the board. Help students find a definition for each word. Have students use each word in a sentence.

"Elizabeth Blackwell"
applying   opportunities
infirmary

"A Night to Remember"
unsinkable   watertight
compartments   lifeboats
bow   stern

Tap Prior Knowledge
"Elizabeth Blackwell": Ask the students if their doctor is a man or a woman. How would they feel if only men could be doctors? Would that be fair?

"A Night to Remember": Ask the students if they have seen a movie about the sinking of the *Titanic*. How would they feel if they were trapped on a sinking ship?

Skill to Emphasize
Review the section about narration of event on page 44. Tell the students that they will try to find the sequence, or order, of events in each article. An event is something that happens. A narration tells about a series of events. The events occur in a certain order, called a sequence.

DURING READING

Preview Text Features
Point out the title of each article. The titles give the students information about the important events they will read about. The title in the Blackwell article also includes the span of years of her life. Point out the words, times, or dates that suggest the sequence in the articles. Boldfaced words indicate vocabulary words.

Point out the dialogue in the *Titanic* article. These words spoken by a person in the event give information and emotions about the event. However, many times such dialogue is fictional. Writers make up what they think someone in history might have said. Students should be able to distinguish what is fictional against a factual background. Many times the words of famous people are recorded. Other times, though, writers simply dramatize a scene from history, and the dialogue is fictional.

Comprehending the Selection
Model how to identify the sequence by asking: *What words or clues tell you the order of events*?

AFTER READING

Reinforce the Comprehension Skill
Tell the students that in most narrations of event, the sequence will be in chronological order. This means the events are presented in the article just as they happen in time. Both articles use chronological order, though the Blackwell article uses years and the *Titanic* article uses hours to present the sequence of events.

Distribute copies of the Sequence Chart on page 120. Have the students complete the chart for both articles. They can use another sheet of paper if necessary.

Assess
Have the students complete the activities for each selection.

WRITE ABOUT IT

Have the students write a paragraph about some accomplishment that made them feel proud.

www.harcourtschoolsupply.com

45

Lesson 8: Teacher Information
Nonfiction Comprehension: Grades 5–6, SV 8948-6

Find the Sequence

Read each paragraph. Darken the circle by the answer that best completes each sentence.

L. Frank Baum was born in New York in 1856, and he died in 1919. He wrote *The Wonderful Wizard of Oz* in 1900. It was made into a musical comedy in 1901.

1. After Baum wrote *The Wonderful Wizard of Oz* in 1900, ____ in 1901.
   - Ⓐ it was made into a movie
   - Ⓑ it was made into a musical comedy
   - Ⓒ it was made into a comic book
   - Ⓓ it was made into a TV show

In 1718, a mission was founded in Texas. It was called the Alamo. The town of San Antonio grew up around it. In 1835 and 1836, a war was fought to free Texas from Mexico. Near the end of that war, a Mexican army of 4,000 attacked 200 Texans inside the Alamo. The battle continued for thirteen days before the brave men inside were killed. After that, "Remember the Alamo" was a battle cry that was shouted as Texans fought for their freedom. Soon Texas was free, and in 1845, it became a state.

2. The battle at the Alamo began when ____.
   - Ⓐ Texas became a state
   - Ⓑ 4,000 Mexicans attacked
   - Ⓒ Texas became free
   - Ⓓ a mission was founded

Many millions of people in Asia follow the teachings of Buddha. Buddha was born in India about 2,500 years ago. His father was a rajah, or king, and Buddha lived a happy, protected childhood in the royal palace. Then, he began leaving the palace and saw the suffering of the people. At the age of 29, he decided to go to the mountains to think about the reason for all of the misery in the world. After a few years, he returned and found peace among the people. For the next 45 years, Buddha walked the land teaching peace and acceptance. Thousands of temples throughout Asia contain statues of the beloved Buddha.

3. After Buddha saw the suffering of the people, he ____.
   - Ⓐ lived a protected childhood
   - Ⓑ found peace among the people
   - Ⓒ began leaving the palace
   - Ⓓ decided to go to the mountains

Nonfiction Comprehension: Grades 5–6, SV 8948-6

Elizabeth Blackwell (1821–1910)

There was a time in this country when women could not be doctors. Elizabeth Blackwell faced this problem, and she became the first woman doctor in the United States.

Blackwell was born in England but moved to New York at age eleven. Although education for girls at that time was mainly in music, sewing, and cooking, Elizabeth's education included math, science, and history.

Blackwell worked as a teacher for a while. But her real goal was to become a doctor. So she began to study medical books. Later she was taught by a doctor. Then she began **applying** to medical schools.

Blackwell soon learned that no medical school wanted a female student. She applied to 29 schools but was not accepted. Finally, she was accepted to the medical school at Geneva College in New York. She graduated in 1849.

Blackwell thought she would have greater **opportunities** to work as a doctor in Europe. She sailed to Europe and worked in England and France.

In 1851 Blackwell returned to New York to practice medicine. Because she was a woman, male doctors refused to accept her as a doctor. She was not allowed to treat patients in any hospitals. Blackwell solved these problems by opening her own hospital in 1857. Her sister Emily, who had also become a doctor, worked with her. Together they started the New York **Infirmary** for Women and Children. It included a medical school to train women to be doctors. Women worked in the hospital, and most of the patients were poor.

Since 1949 an award called the Elizabeth Blackwell Medal has been given to women doctors who have done outstanding work in medicine. This award helps Americans remember that Elizabeth Blackwell made it possible for many other women to become doctors.

Nonfiction Comprehension: Grades 5–6, SV 8948-6

Comprehension and Vocabulary Review

Darken the circle by the best answer.

1. Elizabeth Blackwell graduated from medical school in ____.
   Ⓐ 1849
   Ⓑ 1851
   Ⓒ 1857
   Ⓓ 1949

2. After she graduated from medical school, Blackwell ____.
   Ⓐ opened a sewing shop
   Ⓑ moved to Mexico
   Ⓒ worked as a doctor in Europe
   Ⓓ quit practicing medicine

3. This article is mainly about ____.
   Ⓐ the New York Infirmary for Women and Children
   Ⓑ the Elizabeth Blackwell Medal
   Ⓒ how Elizabeth Blackwell applied to 29 medical schools
   Ⓓ how Elizabeth Blackwell worked to help women become doctors

4. An opportunity is ____.
   Ⓐ a chance to do something
   Ⓑ a kind of sewing stitch
   Ⓒ a musical instrument
   Ⓓ a doctor's uniform

Write About It

Write complete sentences to tell the steps Elizabeth Blackwell took to become a doctor and to help other women become doctors. Use another piece of paper if necessary.

_____

_____

_____

_____

_____

_____

_____

_____

Nonfiction Comprehension: Grades 5–6, SV 8948-6

A Night to Remember

Captain Edward Smith had been given the honor of taking the *Titanic* on her very first trip. After this trip, he planned to retire. Smith told the lookout, Frederick Fleet, about the reports of ice he had received.

"Keep a sharp lookout tonight, Mr. Fleet," the captain said. Then he went inside the ship to eat dinner.

Fleet searched the darkness. His job was to watch for icebergs. Fleet watched carefully, but he wasn't really worried. The *Titanic* was the biggest, strongest, safest ship ever built. All at once, Fleet saw a black shadow right in front of the ship. It was an iceberg! Quickly he rang the warning bell.

"Iceberg!" he screamed. For the next 37 seconds, the crew tried to steer the ship out of the way, but it was no use. At 11:40 P.M. on April 14, 1912, the iceberg rammed the side of the *Titanic*. Slowly, the huge **unsinkable** ship started to sink.

Word of the accident spread quickly through the ship. The passengers were confused but not upset. They thought this was a new adventure. A few crew members knew better.

Captain Smith went to check the 16 **watertight compartments** at the bottom of the ship. The *Titanic* should float even if three or four of them filled with water. Captain Smith found that five of the rooms were now hopelessly flooded. Water was filling the other rooms as well. The *Titanic* was going down.

On the deck, crew members hurried to get out the **lifeboats**, but they had never had a practice drill. It had not seemed necessary. Finally, they got the first boat ready. Captain Smith called out the order.

"Women and children first!"

But most women and children refused to go. They didn't trust the small boats. Many still did not believe the ship was in danger. An hour later, only 20 people were in the first lifeboat. There was room for 45 more people, but the crew could wait no longer. At 12:45 A.M., they lowered the half-empty lifeboat into the water.

Finally, people understood that the *Titanic* was sinking. Suddenly, everyone wanted to get into a lifeboat. But there were not enough to go around. There were 2,207 people on the *Titanic*, but there were only enough lifeboats for 1,178 people.

    Nonfiction Comprehension: Grades 5–6, SV 8948-6

The shortage of lifeboats brought out the worst in some people. One man snuck into a lifeboat dressed as a woman. Others pushed ahead of mothers and small children. Some men had to be dragged kicking and screaming out of the boats.

But while some people became cowards, others became heroes.

Dr. W.T. Minahan helped his wife into a boat, then stepped back to make room for someone else. "Be brave," he called to his wife. "No matter what happens, be brave."

Someone else tried to help an older man named Isidor Straus into a lifeboat. But Straus shook his head. Mrs. Straus, like many other women, refused to leave her husband. "We have been living together for many years," she said. "Where you go, I go." Then the two of them sat down in deck chairs to wait for the end together.

On the deck, the ship's band played on. They felt it was their duty to stay with the ship. They tried to comfort the passengers by playing loud, cheerful music.

By 2:00 A.M., all of the lifeboats were in the water. There wasn't much hope left for those still on the ship. Some jumped into the water and tried to swim out to the lifeboats. A few made it, but most quickly died in the freezing water.

One swimmer looked back and saw Captain Smith standing on the ship with water up to his waist. The **bow** of the ship was underwater, and the **stern** was up in the air. At 2:18 A.M., with the band still playing, the great ship sank to the bottom of the ocean, taking more than 1,500 people with it.

"Mayday, mayday!" The *Titanic's* radio operator called for help on the ship's radio. The *Carpathia* was the first ship to arrive. Its crew began picking up the people in the lifeboats at 4:10 A.M. Of the 2,207 people who had sailed on the *Titanic*, only 711 were still alive.

The *Titanic* became a legend. For 73 years, people searched for its remains. Finally, on September 1, 1985, a team of French and American explorers found her. The rusty wreck lay two miles under the Atlantic Ocean. She was no longer the beautiful and graceful ship she had once been.

Name _____ **Date** _____

Comprehension and Vocabulary Review

 Darken the circle by the best answer.

1. The captain of the *Titanic* was ____.
   Ⓐ W.T. Minahan
   Ⓑ Frederick Fleet
   Ⓒ Isidor Straus
   Ⓓ Edward Smith

2. The *Titanic* sank after it hit ____.
   Ⓐ another ship
   Ⓑ an iceberg
   Ⓒ a storm
   Ⓓ a big tree

3. This article is mainly about ____.
   Ⓐ the sinking of the *Titanic*
   Ⓑ how the wreck of the *Titanic* was found
   Ⓒ heroes and cowards on the *Titanic*
   Ⓓ the captain of the *Titanic*

4. A compartment is ____.
   Ⓐ a kind of food
   Ⓑ a small room
   Ⓒ a computer
   Ⓓ a kind of lifeboat

5. You can conclude that a watertight compartment should ____.
   Ⓐ be made of paper
   Ⓑ keep water out
   Ⓒ sink
   Ⓓ not be used in a ship

6. Many people did not worry after the accident because ____.
   Ⓐ they thought it was all a big joke
   Ⓑ they were too busy eating
   Ⓒ they liked the song the band was playing
   Ⓓ they thought the *Titanic* was unsinkable

7. The first rescue ship to arrive was ____.
   Ⓐ *Old Ironsides*
   Ⓑ the *Carpathia*
   Ⓒ the *Queen Mary*
   Ⓓ the *Nautilus*

8. If the bow is the front of a ship, the stern must be ____.
   Ⓐ the bottom of the ship
   Ⓑ the anchor of the ship
   Ⓒ the rear of the ship
   Ⓓ the captain's quarters

Nonfiction Comprehension: Grades 5–6, SV 8948-6

Sequence Review

The sequence of events is the order in which the events occur. Often, times or dates are used to help you understand the sequence. In this article, a time is used to tell when each event occurred.

➡ **Reread the article. Then write complete sentences to describe the event that occurred at each time.**

April 14, 1912

11:40 P.M. _____

_____

_____

April 15, 1912

12:45 A.M. _____

_____

_____

2:00 A.M. _____

_____

_____

2:18 A.M. _____

_____

_____

4:10 A.M. _____

_____

_____

LESSON 9

BEFORE READING

SELECTION DETAILS

Summary
"Find the Sequence" (page 54): The sample paragraphs give practice in identifying the sequence in short selections.

"How to Figure a Batting Average" (page 55): This article tells the students how to figure a batting average in baseball.

"How Does a Power Plant Make Electricity?" (page 56): This article is an informational narration of process that tells how electricity is generated in a power plant.

Selection Type
Mathematics Article
Science Article

Comprehension Skill
Identify Sequence of Events in a Narration of Process

Standards
Reading
• Identify the order of steps in a reading selection.
• Use features of a reading selection such as lists, diagrams, subheadings, and maps.

Mathematics
• Calculate averages using whole numbers and decimals.

Science
• Explore an industry's use of science and technology.

VOCABULARY

Introduce the vocabulary words for each article. Write the words on the board. Help students find a definition for each word. Have students use each word in a sentence.

"How to Figure a Batting Average"
accuracy   stances

"How Does a Power Plant Make Electricity?"
insulated   current
turbine   generator

Tap Prior Knowledge
"How to Figure a Batting Average": Ask the students if they watch baseball games. Do they know how to figure a batting average?

"How Does a Power Plant Make Electricity?": Ask the students what electrical machines they use each day. Do they know how electricity is made to run those machines?

Skill to Emphasize
Review the section about narration of process on page 44. Tell the students that they will try to find the sequence, or order, of steps in each article. A process is a way in which something is done, such as baking a cake or generating electricity.

DURING READING

Preview Text Features
Point out the titles of the articles on pages 55 and 56. The titles give the students information about the process they will read about. Point out the diagram in "How Does a Power Plant Make Electricity?" Point out the picture of Ted Williams in "How to Figure a Batting Average." Williams was a famous baseball player. Boldfaced words in the articles indicate vocabulary words.

Comprehending the Selection
Model how to identify the sequence by asking: *What words or clues tell you the order of steps in the process?*

AFTER READING

Reinforce the Comprehension Skill
Tell the students that in a narration of process, the sequence will be in chronological order. The steps in a how-to are presented in the order they should be done.

Distribute copies of the Sequence Chart on page 120. Have the students complete the chart for "How Does a Power Plant Make Electricity?" They can use another sheet of paper if necessary.

Assess
Have the students complete the activities for each selection.

WRITE ABOUT IT

Have the students write a how-to process about something they know how to do well.

AT HOME

Have the students find the batting average of their favorite player in the newspaper or on the Internet. Have them bring the information to share with the class.

Nonfiction Comprehension: Grades 5–6, SV 8948-6

Find the Sequence

Read each paragraph. Darken the circle by the answer that best completes each sentence.

Sedimentary rocks are formed by the building up of layers of material on the bottom of lakes and oceans. First, sand, gravel, and mud are washed into the lake or ocean from the land. At the same time, the bodies of dead animals fall to the floor of the lakes and oceans. These materials form thick layers on the bottom. The layers then stick together and eventually become sedimentary rock.

1. Right before the materials become rock, they ____.
   Ⓐ are washed into the lake
   Ⓑ stick together
   Ⓒ form thick layers
   Ⓓ become sedimentary rock

Measles is a common childhood disease. Adults can get the measles, but most people have already had it before they become adults. It begins when a person is exposed to a tiny germ called a virus. Eleven days later, the person seems to be getting a cold and might have a headache and a runny nose. In a few days, a fever develops, and then a rash breaks out. Fortunately, there is now a vaccine that is given to children to prevent them from getting measles.

2. The first sign of measles is ____.
   Ⓐ a rash
   Ⓑ a fever
   Ⓒ a vaccine
   Ⓓ a cold

In the spring, robins fly north after having spent the winter in a warmer climate. They select a place for a nest. It may be quite near a house because robins don't seem to mind being in full view of humans. They then collect sticks, leaves, and grass to build a strong nest. After the nest is completed, the female robin lays from three to five blue eggs. When the eggs hatch, the baby robins keep their parents busy feeding them worms and insects. They have feathers in ten days but don't have the parents' bright orange breast until later.

3. After the eggs hatch, the robins ____.
   Ⓐ feed the hungry babies
   Ⓑ fly north in the spring
   Ⓒ collect sticks, leaves, and grass
   Ⓓ select a place for a nest

54

Name _____ Date _____

How to Figure a Batting Average

In baseball, a player's batting average is the number of safe hits he has divided by the number of times he has tried to hit the ball. The number is represented in thousandths for greater **accuracy**. For example, suppose a batter has 50 attempts (at-bats) and gets 17 hits. To find the batting average, you would divide 17 by 50. The batting average would be $\frac{17}{50}$ or .340.

 Write an answer for each question.

1. When a batter has 12 hits in 50 at-bats, what is his batting average?

   _____

2. If a batter has an average of .420 after 50 at-bats, how many hits did he have? (Hint: To find the number of hits, multiply the batting average by the number of at-bats.)

   _____

3. The same batter's average drops to .400 after 25 more at-bats. How many hits did he get in those additional 25 at-bats?

   _____

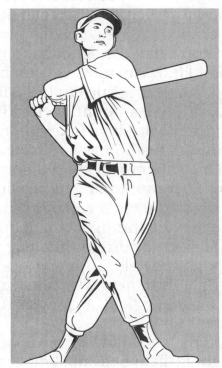

Ted Williams was the last man to bat over .400 in a complete Major League season. He did it in 1941.

There are a few batters who can hit the ball from both right-handed and left-handed **stances**. These batters are called switch-hitters. Switch-hitters keep averages for both sides to see from which side they hit better. A batter might hit .300 left-handed and .350 right-handed. His total batting average would be $\frac{.300 + .350}{2}$, or .325.

A switch-hitter is batting .320 right-handed after 50 at-bats. He decides to start batting left-handed. After another 50 at-bats, his overall average is .360.

4. How many hits did he get left-handed? _____

5. What was his left-handed batting average? _____

Nonfiction Comprehension: Grades 5–6, SV 8948-6

How Does a Power Plant Make Electricity?

You probably know that electricity flows from a power plant to your home through special **insulated** wires. To understand how a power plant produces electricity, you can do a simple experiment. All you need is a wire and a magnet. You know that a magnet has a magnetic field around it. If you move a wire through that magnetic field, an electric current flows in the wire. You can make a small amount of electricity. But a power plant must produce much more electricity to supply all the homes and factories in a town or city.

One wire moving past a magnet can make a very weak **current**. Adding more wires makes the current stronger. A coil of one hundred loops of wire moving through a magnetic field produces more electric current than one wire moving through the field. To keep the electric current flowing, the coil of wire must continue to move in the magnetic field. As long as the coil moves, the current flows.

A small coil of wire moving through the magnetic field of a small magnet makes a weak electric current for a short time. An electric power plant must produce a very strong current. The power plant uses flowing water or steam and special machines to make a large, strong electric current. The water or steam spins the blades of a huge fan called a **turbine**. As the turbine's blades spin, they turn a large coil of wire. The coil of wire moves through the magnetic field of a giant, ring-shaped magnet inside a **generator**. The many loops of the huge coil spin very fast in the middle of the magnet. The coil never leaves the magnetic field. Together, the giant magnet and the huge, spinning coil make a strong, steady electric current. A power plant has many generators to produce the electricity you use at school and home.

Electric Generator

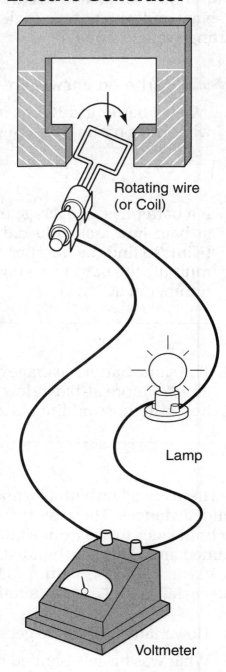

Rotating wire (or Coil)

Lamp

Voltmeter

As the wire spins through the magnetic field, an electric current flows through the wire.

Name _____ Date_____

Comprehension and Vocabulary Review

 Darken the circle by the best answer.

1. Electric current will flow in a wire that moves through a ____ field.
   - Ⓐ football
   - Ⓑ wire
   - Ⓒ magnetic
   - Ⓓ hay

2. A power plant uses flowing water or ____ to produce electricity.
   - Ⓐ ice
   - Ⓑ snow
   - Ⓒ eels
   - Ⓓ steam

3. This article is mainly about ____.
   - Ⓐ how to use magnets many different ways
   - Ⓑ how a power plant generates electricity
   - Ⓒ how to wind wire around a nail
   - Ⓓ what a turbine looks like

4. In a power plant, the magnet used to produce electricity is called ____.
   - Ⓐ an electricity machine
   - Ⓑ a coil
   - Ⓒ a current
   - Ⓓ a generator

Briefly summarize how a power plant generates electricity. Write complete sentences.

_____

_____

_____

_____

_____

_____

_____

_____

_____

_____

Nonfiction Comprehension: Grades 5–6, SV 8948-6

Cause and Effect

BEFORE READING

Tap Prior Knowledge
"Tsunami!": Ask the students if they have ever seen big waves at the beach. Do they like to play in the waves? What would happen if those waves were 200 feet tall and moving at 500 miles per hour?

Skill to Emphasize
Review the section about cause and effect on page 44. Tell the students that many things that happen are caused by other things. What happens is an effect. What causes it to happen is a cause. Sometimes an effect then becomes a cause.

DURING READING

Preview Text Features
Point out the subtitles in the "Tsunami!" article. They tell about the cause-effect relationship. Have the students look out for signal words that indicate a cause-effect relationship. Boldfaced words in the article indicate vocabulary words.

Comprehending the Selection
Model how to identify causes and effects by asking: *What is one thing that happened in the article? What caused that thing to happen?*

AFTER READING

Reinforce the Comprehension Skill
Tell the students that in cause-effect relationships, one cause can have many effects, and one effect can have many causes. Students should think about why things happen, then be able to identify the cause of events or the effects of causes.

Distribute copies of the Cause-Effect Chart on page 121. Have the students complete the chart for the articles.

Assess
Have the students complete the activities for each selection.

WRITE ABOUT IT

Have the students write about something that happened to them recently. Have them identify the causes of what happened.

SELECTION DETAILS

Summary
"Find the Cause or Effect" (page 59): The sample paragraphs give practice in identifying causes and effects in short selections.

"Tsunami!" (page 61): This article tells the causes and effects of the giant waves called tsunamis.

Selection Type
Science Article

Comprehension Skill
Identify Cause and Effect

Standards
Reading
• Understand cause and effect in a factual article.

Science
• Describe how earthquakes and floods affect human activities.

VOCABULARY

Introduce the vocabulary words for the "Tsunami!" article. Write the words on the board. Help students find a definition for each word. Have students use each word in a sentence.

tsunami	disturbances
seismic	meteorites
crests	troughs
phenomenon	complex
predict	analyze

Find the Cause or Effect

➡ **Darken the circle by the best answer.**

The hamster is a popular pet in the United States. It was first brought here to use in experiments. Because it was so cute, it quickly became a pet in many homes. Sometimes it stuffs its cheek pockets full of food, and as a result, it looks as if it has the mumps. Hamsters multiply rapidly because the females can have babies when only three or four months old.

1. The hamster became a pet in many homes because it ____.
   Ⓐ was so cute
   Ⓑ cost little
   Ⓒ ate little
   Ⓓ had pockets

2. Because the hamster stuffs its cheek pockets with food, it ____.
   Ⓐ frightens many people
   Ⓑ can get very sick
   Ⓒ is used in experiments
   Ⓓ seems to have the mumps

Robert Louis Stevenson was a famous author who was born in Scotland. He had studied to be an engineer and a lawyer. He wasn't able to do those things because of poor health. He began to write for magazines instead. He wrote *Treasure Island* because he wanted to entertain his young stepson. He also wrote *Kidnapped* and *The Strange Case of Dr. Jekyll and Mr. Hyde*. He died in the Samoan Islands. The natives honored him; and, as a result, they buried him as they would a chief. They called him "teller of tales."

3. Because of poor health, Robert Louis Stevenson ____.
   Ⓐ wanted to entertain his stepson
   Ⓑ couldn't be an engineer or lawyer
   Ⓒ was called "teller of tales"
   Ⓓ wrote *Treasure Island*

4. The natives buried Robert Louis Stevenson as a chief because he ____.
   Ⓐ wrote *Kidnapped*
   Ⓑ was a lawyer
   Ⓒ was born in Samoa
   Ⓓ was honored by them

Name _____ Date_____

➡ **Darken the circle by the best answer.**

Over 2,000 years ago, Plato said there had been another continent called Atlantis. He said it had sunk because of an earthquake. Scientists haven't found any evidence that Plato's idea is true, so it is considered by most people to be untrue. Some people, however, continue to believe in Atlantis.

5. Plato said that Atlantis sank because of ____.
   Ⓐ volcanic eruptions
   Ⓑ too little evidence
   Ⓒ an earthquake
   Ⓓ a solar eclipse

6. Because scientists haven't found any evidence, they ____.
   Ⓐ continue looking for proof
   Ⓑ call Plato a liar
   Ⓒ study earthquakes
   Ⓓ believe the idea is untrue

Stephen Douglas was the man defeated by Abraham Lincoln in the presidential election of 1860. He was known as "The Little Giant" because he was a small man with a very big head. In 1858, Douglas had defeated Lincoln and was elected to the Senate because the voters liked his ideas better than Lincoln's. He offered to help Lincoln after Lincoln became President. Since Douglas died soon after that, he never had the chance to give his help.

7. Douglas defeated Lincoln in the 1858 election because ____.
   Ⓐ no one knew Abraham Lincoln
   Ⓑ many voters stayed home
   Ⓒ people liked his ideas
   Ⓓ Lincoln didn't want to win

8. Since Douglas was a small man with a very big head, he ____.
   Ⓐ stood on a platform to speak
   Ⓑ was called "The Little Giant"
   Ⓒ lost the Presidential election
   Ⓓ offered to help Lincoln

Nonfiction Comprehension: Grades 5–6, SV 8948-6

Tsunami!

A **tsunami** (soo NAH mee) is a gigantic, powerful ocean wave. Tsunamis are sometimes called tidal waves, but this term is incorrect. Tides do not cause tsunamis.

The word *tsunami* comes from the Japanese words for harbor (*tsu-*) and sea (*-nami*). Tsunamis can form far out in the ocean, but they are most dangerous when they make it to shore. Tsunamis can kill people and animals. They can flood villages and farmland. They can cause terrible damage.

Scientists are learning how to predict tsunamis. Still, these giant waves often strike without warning. In July 1998, for example, a tsunami struck the coast of Papua, New Guinea. There was no warning. People could not escape. Villages were destroyed.

What Causes Them?

Tsunamis are caused by **disturbances** deep within the ocean. These are called **seismic** disturbances. They have to do with vibrations in the earth. Seismic disturbances include earthquakes, volcanoes, landslides, and explosions. **Meteorites** can also cause tsunamis. A meteorite is a mass of metal or stone that has fallen to Earth.

Earthquakes under the ocean floor cause most tsunamis. When an earthquake happens in the ocean, its energy is transferred to the water. Waves spread outward in circles. In deep water, these waves may only be about 1 or 2 feet (0.3 or 0.6 meters) tall. If you were in a ship in the middle of the ocean, you could even pass over a tsunami without ever noticing it.

How a Tsunami Is Formed

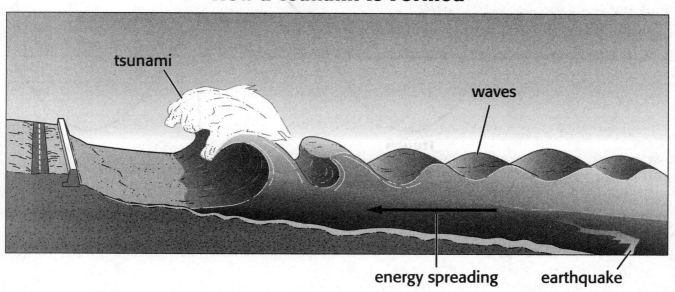

tsunami

waves

energy spreading

earthquake

Nonfiction Comprehension: Grades 5–6, SV 8948-6

As a tsunami approaches land, however, it becomes much more ominous. The wave gets taller. Even though the wave may have traveled great distances, it has not lost much energy. It rushes toward land at speeds of up to 500 miles (805 kilometers) per hour. By the time it strikes shore, the tsunami may be nearly 200 feet (61 meters) tall!

Tsunami Tragedies

Like all waves, tsunamis have **crests** and **troughs**. In 1755, a tsunami hit the shore off Lisbon, Portugal. The trough struck first. As a result, the shallow floor of the bay was exposed. It was as if someone had pulled the plug on a bathtub. The people of Lisbon had never seen such an amazing sight, so they crowded onto the dry sea floor. Minutes later, the wave crest arrived. Water poured back into the bay, drowning many of the people.

Another tsunami tragedy occurred in 1883. A volcano erupted on the island of Krakatau in Indonesia. Much of the island was destroyed by the explosion. Then the resulting tsunamis killed more than 36,000 people on other islands in the area.

The largest tsunami ever measured was off the coast of Japan in 1971. It was 279 feet (85 meters) high. One of the most destructive tsunamis was also in Japan. It occurred in 1703 and killed over 100,000 people. It is no wonder that the Japanese created a word for this **phenomenon**.

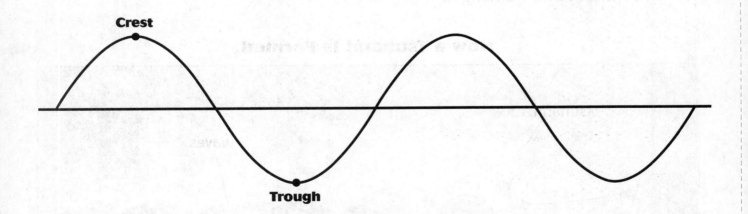

Crest

Trough

Predicting Tsunamis

Tsunamis are **complex**. Many factors affect their movements. These factors include wave speed, wave height, wind conditions, and the shapes of seabeds and coastlines. Sometimes a tsunami will approach an island from one direction. Then it will bend around and hit the other side. For these reasons, it is difficult to **predict** where and when tsunamis will strike.

It is also difficult to predict the effect of tsunamis because they can travel so far. In 1960, for example, an earthquake occurred off South America that sent waves rushing in many directions across the Pacific Ocean. Huge waves caused destruction on many islands in the Pacific, including Hawaii. Then just 22 hours later, a tsunami slammed into Japan. If scientists could have predicted the path of the big wave, many lives could have been saved.

Scientists now use computers to **analyze** tsunamis. They are learning where these deadly waves are likely to strike. They are also learning how to track them. In the future, scientists hope to warn people when a tsunami is coming so they can get out of its way.

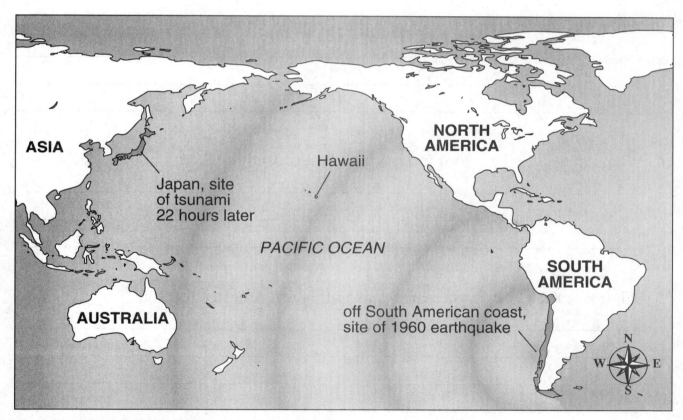

ASIA

Japan, site of tsunami 22 hours later

Hawaii

NORTH AMERICA

PACIFIC OCEAN

AUSTRALIA

off South American coast, site of 1960 earthquake

SOUTH AMERICA

N W E S

The 1960 tsunami traveled westward across the Pacific Ocean and struck Hawaii and then Japan.

Nonfiction Comprehension: Grades 5–6, SV 8948-6

Name _____ Date _____

Comprehension Review

→ **Write complete sentences to answer each question.**

1. What causes tsunamis?

_____

_____

_____

2. What are some of the effects of a tsunami?

_____

_____

_____

3. What was the effect of the volcano that erupted on Krakatau in 1883?

_____

_____

_____

4. What caused the bay floor in Lisbon to be exposed in 1755?

_____

_____

_____

5. What was the effect of the earthquake off South America in 1960?

_____

_____

_____

_____

_____

_____

Nonfiction Comprehension: Grades 5–6, SV 8948-6

Vocabulary Review

 Darken the circle by the best answer.

1. In this article, a tsunami is ____.
   Ⓐ a terrible storm
   Ⓑ an earthquake
   Ⓒ a large, powerful wave
   Ⓓ a vibration from Earth

2. In this article, meteorites are ____.
   Ⓐ chunks of debris from space
   Ⓑ materials from volcanoes
   Ⓒ high winds
   Ⓓ large boats

3. In this article, a phenomenon is ____.
   Ⓐ a dangerous storm
   Ⓑ a word created by the Japanese
   Ⓒ an enormous, powerful wave
   Ⓓ an unusual fact or event

4. In this article, crests are ____.
   Ⓐ the high tops of waves
   Ⓑ the low spaces between waves
   Ⓒ the middle parts of waves
   Ⓓ large waves

5. In this article, troughs are ____.
   Ⓐ the high tops of waves
   Ⓑ the low spaces between waves
   Ⓒ the middle parts of waves
   Ⓓ large waves

6. In this article, *seismic* means ____.
   Ⓐ related to tides
   Ⓑ related to vibrations in the earth
   Ⓒ the movement of waves
   Ⓓ related to outer space

Build Your Vocabulary

Synonyms are words that have the same meaning or almost the same meaning.

 Write the synonym from the box for each underlined word.

> disturbances   complex   ominous   analyze

7. The scientists made sure to <u>study</u> their data carefully. _____

8. <u>Threatening</u> waves pounded the shore. _____

9. I struggled to complete the <u>difficult</u> math assignment. _____

10. A ringing phone caused <u>interruptions</u> in the play. _____

Nonfiction Comprehension: Grades 5–6, SV 8948-6

UNIT 4 Description

Description is concerned with the relationship between the whole and its parts. It can be used to provide physical description, in which details of a person, place, or object are presented to appeal to the reader's senses. It also can be used for division, to identify the component parts that make up the whole of something. In both these forms, the function of description is to demonstrate how the parts work together to produce the whole.

• Physical Description (Lesson 11)

Students use physical description on a daily basis to characterize the things around them. They might say, "I ate a juicy orange for lunch" or "The cold ice cream made my tongue tingle" or "We got a new blue car." Each of these descriptions gives physical details about an object. By using these physical details, the writer appeals to the reader's senses. The more of the reader's senses that are brought into play, the more effective is the physical description.

A good physical description will downplay the common features to show the uniqueness of the subject. An assumption is made that all people have two arms or two ears or a nose. Lack of these things would be a kind of uniqueness. Unusual features, such as a long nose, would also be a sign of uniqueness. The details that distinguish one person from another, for example, are the unique features, not the common ones. By showing both common and unique features, description becomes very important in mastering the later skill of classification.

The more thorough the description, the more effectively a sense of the whole is achieved. If a writer says a room has a door and two windows, the reader gets a rough sense of the thing being described. By adding details about the parts, the sense of the whole is more completely realized. As the writer provides more details and a more effective whole, the reader more easily experiences the thing being described.

To get the most information from a physical description:

- First, identify the thing being described (for example, a building).
- Look for details about parts of the thing (for example, doors, windows, walls, roof).
- Look for words that appeal to the senses of sight, smell, taste, touch, and hearing.
- Put all the details together to get the whole picture.
- Try to draw a picture of the thing on paper or in your mind.
- Decide how the thing described is unique or different from other things.
- Try to write a summary description of the thing.

• Division—Writing About Parts (Lesson 12)

Like physical description, division is a form of organization that shows how the various parts make up the whole. Division is not the same as classification. Division shows the parts of the whole, whereas classification puts things into different groups. Classification would put the school building into *kinds* of buildings, but division would discuss the *parts* of the school building.

Physical description is often a part of division. The parts of the whole are described. However, the main focus of division is to identify the parts that are used to create the whole. You might ask the students, "What are the parts of the classroom?" or "What are the parts of a book?" Using the organizational skill of division, the students can more easily see how the parts work together to create the object.

To get the most information from an article of division:

- First, identify the topic being discussed (for example, the parts of a plant).
- Look for descriptive details about the parts (for example, stem, petals, leaves).
- Pay attention to what each part does in relation to the whole (for example, the stem holds up the plant).
- Put all the parts together to produce the whole thing.
- Try to draw a picture of the thing on paper or in your mind.
- Highlight each part in your picture.
- Try to write a summary that tells how the parts work together to make up the whole thing.

Research Base

"Content literacy involves knowing what to expect—anticipating the kinds of organizational structures the reader might encounter. Content literacy also involves understanding the kinds of graphic features the reader needs to interpret, as well as vocabulary specific to the topic. The reader uses the text's organization, language, and visual features in a unified way to derive meaning. In other words students must learn how to read history, biology, environmental science, geographical descriptions, and other kinds of texts." (*Guiding Readers and Writers: Grades 3–6*, p. 400)

LESSON 11

Physical Description

SELECTION DETAILS

Summary
"Find the Descriptive Details" (page 68): The sample paragraphs give practice in identifying descriptive details in short selections.

"Cockroaches" (page 69): This article gives descriptive details about the appearance and behavior of the common cockroach.

"Shackleton" (page 70): This article narrates with descriptive details the misadventures of Sir Ernest Shackleton and his crew in their quest to cross Antarctica on foot.

Selection Type
Science Article
Social Studies Article

Comprehension Skill
Identify Sensory Words in Descriptive Article

Standards
Reading
• Identify words that appeal to the senses.
• Identify details in a reading selection.

Science
• Based on attributes, place living organisms into groups based on similarities.

Social Studies
• Put in chronological order important people and events.

VOCABULARY

Introduce the vocabulary words for each article. Write the words on the board. Help students find a definition for each word. Have students use each word in a sentence.

"Cockroaches"
antennae

"Shackleton"

floes	*fatigued*
launch	*frostbite*
raging	*ached*
toil	*apprehensive*

Tap Prior Knowledge
"Cockroaches": Ask the students what they know about this common pest. Have they seen one today? Have the students draw a cockroach.

"Shackleton": Ask the students what they know about Antarctica. Would they like to walk across it? What sort of problems do they think they might encounter?

Skill to Emphasize
Review the section about physical description on page 66. Tell the students that good writers use words that appeal to the reader's senses of sight, smell, taste, touch, and hearing. Sensory words make the writing more interesting and vivid.

DURING READING

Preview Text Features
Point out the title of each article. The titles give the students information about the things that will be described. Have the students look at the illustrations to get a better idea of what is being described. Boldfaced words indicate vocabulary words.

Comprehending the Selection
Model a better understanding of physical description by asking: *What words in the article appeal to your senses of sight, smell, taste, touch, and hearing?*

AFTER READING

Reinforce the Comprehension Skill
Tell the students that a good description helps them to see an object clearly in their mind. Ask the students to point out words in "Cockroaches" and "Shackleton" that allow them to see pictures clearly in their mind. What are some of the pictures they can see in their mind after reading the articles?

Assess
Have the students complete the activities for each selection.

WRITE ABOUT IT

Have the students write a description about a person, place, or thing that they like. Tell them to be sure to use sensory words.

AT HOME

Have students look in the newspaper or news magazines for articles that contain descriptions and bring the articles to school to share with the class.

Find the Descriptive Details

➡️ **Read each paragraph. Darken the circle by the best answer.**

Poison ivy is a common, poisonous plant. It has three leaflets on each stem and white berries. Poison ivy can grow as a bush or as a vine. Its leaves are green and shiny in the summer. In the fall, they are a beautiful shade of red. Some people can have a severe reaction if they come into contact with any part of the plant. The poisonous juice is present in the leaves, stem, and flowers. Many people think that any plant with three leaves and white berries should be avoided to prevent possible poisoning.

1. The poison ivy plant has ____ berries.
   Ⓐ red
   Ⓑ three
   Ⓒ white
   Ⓓ green

Moose are the largest of all antlered animals. The Alaskan moose is the largest moose of all, some weighing as much as 1,800 pounds. Some Alaskan bull moose have been measured at $7\frac{1}{2}$ feet at the shoulder. Their antlers reach to 10 feet above the ground. These antlers can weigh 95 pounds and reach widths of 6 feet and more.

2. The antlers of a bull moose can weigh ____ pounds.
   Ⓐ 1,800
   Ⓑ 10
   Ⓒ 6
   Ⓓ 95

There are three main types of clouds. The big, fluffy ones are called cumulus clouds. *Cumulus* means "pile," and this type of cloud may reach up several miles from its base to its top. Another type is the stratus cloud. *Stratus* means "layer," and stratus clouds make a low, gray layer. *Cirrus* means "curl." Cirrus clouds are feathery and often look like curls of smoke.

3. Cirrus clouds look like ____.
   Ⓐ fluffy cotton
   Ⓑ curls of smoke
   Ⓒ a low, gray layer
   Ⓓ a big tree

Crater Lake is in the crater of a dead volcano. Its sides are covered with evergreens, and its water is a bright blue. The lake is about 2,000 feet deep. It is the deepest lake in the United States. The sides of the crater rise 2,000 feet above the lake's surface.

4. The water in Crater Lake is ____.
   Ⓐ hot
   Ⓑ green
   Ⓒ blue
   Ⓓ made of lava

Nonfiction Comprehension: Grades 5–6, SV 8948-6

Cockroaches

Cockroaches are insects. There are many kinds of cockroaches. Some kinds can fly. Roaches are kitchen pests in warm climates. They leave many droppings, or wastes. Cockroaches can carry germs. As far as we know, cockroaches do not spread disease.

Roaches come out at night. They use **antennae**, or feelers, for a sense of touch and smell. They will eat any kind of food. They also eat paper, cloth, ink, and even shoe polish.

The German cockroach is found all over the world. This cockroach is about $\frac{1}{2}$ inch long. It is yellow-brown and has wings. The American cockroach is about $1\frac{1}{2}$ inches long. It is brown and can fly.

Keeping cockroaches out of houses is not easy. The best way is to keep the kitchen clean. Wash dishes before going to bed. Don't leave food around. Don't leave paper bags in corners where cockroaches can hide.

antennae

 Darken the circle by the best answer.

1. According to the article, the American cockroach is ____.
   Ⓐ $\frac{1}{2}$ inch long and yellow-brown
   Ⓑ $\frac{1}{2}$ inch long and brown
   Ⓒ $1\frac{1}{2}$ inches long and black
   Ⓓ $1\frac{1}{2}$ inches long and brown

2. According to the article, the German cockroach ____.
   Ⓐ eats shoes
   Ⓑ spreads disease
   Ⓒ is yellow-brown and has wings
   Ⓓ is brown and can fly

Write a complete sentence to answer the question.

3. What do roaches smell with? _____

_____

Nonfiction Comprehension: Grades 5–6, SV 8948-6

Shackleton

On December 23, 1915, Sir Ernest Shackleton and his 27 men began the long journey across the frozen ocean. As they moved along, they saw only huge slabs of ice in all directions. With each step, they broke through the top layer and freezing water washed around their knees.

Shackleton saw the men struggling. He called one man over to him. "We may not live through this march," he said. "Leave this note back at our camp. Perhaps someday someone will find it. Then the world will know what happened to us."

In December 1914, Sir Ernest and his team had set sail for Antarctica. They had hoped to be the first people to cross the frozen continent on foot. They never reached land, however. Their ship had gotten stuck in ice. For nine months they had been trapped, surrounded by huge slabs of ice called **floes**. Finally the ice tore the ship apart, and the group had been forced to leave it. "And so here we are, 200 miles from the nearest island," Shackleton thought, "and 1,000 miles from the nearest humans."

After five days of marching, Sir Ernest told the men to stop. They had gone only ten miles, and they were greatly **fatigued** from the march.

"We will find a solid ice floe and pitch our tents," he announced. "Then we will wait. When the ice breaks up, we will **launch** the lifeboats."

For three months they waited. Day after day the wind whipped their faces. The temperature dipped to below zero. Food supplies ran low. The men grew worried.

"Don't give up hope," Sir Ernest told them. "Remember, every day we float closer to Elephant Island."

Elephant Island was nothing but a large rock. To Shackleton's men, however, it was the only hope. Past the island lay 3,000 miles of open ocean. By April 8, 1916, the ice was splitting up. Sharp pieces of ice filled the water, so Shackleton didn't want to launch the lifeboats, but that night their ice floe cracked into two pieces, and the men just had time to jump onto one half before the other half drifted out of reach. The next day, they launched the boats.

Now, the men had new problems. The wind grew stronger, and waves 30 feet high sprayed freezing water into the boats. **Frostbite**, hunger, and thirst also weakened them. One man noted in his diary, "No sleep for 48 hours. All wet and cold with a blizzard **raging**."

For five days and nights, they sat in the three small boats. The salt water gave them bleeding sores all over their bodies. Their arms **ached** from rowing. Their toes ached from the cold. Sir Ernest suffered as much as anyone, but he never let it show. He stood at the front of one boat, searching for Elephant Island. The wind cut into him, and the water soaked him. Still, he stayed at his post.

"He is a wonderful man," wrote one man. "He simply never spares himself if, by his **toil**, he can possibly help anyone else."

At last Elephant Island appeared in the distance. Like the others, Shackleton was happy to be on dry land. But the island could not support life. No ship ever came to Elephant Island, so there was no hope of being found there.

"I am going to try to sail across the ocean to South Georgia," he told his crew. "I need five men to come with me."

On April 24, the six men rowed away from Elephant Island. They had to cross 800 miles of open ocean in a 22-foot boat. This stretch of ocean, called Cape Horn, is the stormiest in the world. The men who stayed behind were **apprehensive**. They feared the boat wouldn't make it, and they feared they would die on Elephant Island.

In open waters, the boat moved swiftly, but every minute and a half the boat was lifted onto 50-foot waves. As it crashed back down into the water, the men held on to the sides so they wouldn't be washed overboard. Winds roared at them at 80 miles per hour. Their drinking water ran out, and their tongues became swollen from thirst.

After two weeks, they neared the island of South Georgia, and at last, on May 8, they caught sight of the islands. Even after they landed, their journey was not over. All the people lived on the other side of the island. Shackleton left the three weakest men on the shore. He and the two others set out to walk the 29 miles to the town of Stromness. They clawed their way up mountains 4,500 feet high. They stumbled along frozen rocks and slid down steep cliffs. At last, on May 20, they reached Stromness. They were weak, frostbitten, and dangerously thin. But they were alive.

Quickly a ship was sent to get the three men on the other side of South Georgia. They were picked up easily, but bad weather kept ships from getting to Elephant Island. At last, on August 30, 1916, Shackleton landed a ship there. To his joy, he found all 22 men still alive. The group had seen amazingly rough times. But every single man came out alive.

Name _____ Date_____

Comprehension and Vocabulary Review

➤ **Darken the circle by the best answer.**

1. Shackleton was trying to ____.
   Ⓐ find the North Pole
   Ⓑ cross Antarctica
   Ⓒ circle the globe
   Ⓓ find the source of the Amazon

2. Elephant Island was ____.
   Ⓐ nothing but a large rock
   Ⓑ hot
   Ⓒ covered with trees
   Ⓓ full of elephants

3. You can conclude that Shackleton left Elephant Island because ____.
   Ⓐ his men no longer trusted him
   Ⓑ he was going back to Antarctica
   Ⓒ he was dying
   Ⓓ he wanted to get help for his men

4. Shackleton and five other men crossed Cape Horn ____.
   Ⓐ on an ice floe
   Ⓑ in a small boat
   Ⓒ on a mountain
   Ⓓ in an airplane

➤ A description includes words that appeal to the senses. Write a description about one part of Shackleton's adventures—the sinking of the ship by the ice floes, the journey around Cape Horn in the small boat, the trek across the mountains of South Georgia Island, or the men left behind on Elephant Island. Include descriptive details about the weather and the ice. Write complete sentences. Use another piece of paper if necessary.

_____
_____
_____
_____
_____
_____
_____
_____
_____

Vocabulary Review

Darken the circle by the best meaning of the underlined word.

1. They were greatly <u>fatigued</u> by the march.
   - Ⓐ frozen
   - Ⓑ tired
   - Ⓒ made overweight
   - Ⓓ saddened

2. Shackleton <u>launched</u> the boats.
   - Ⓐ put into the water
   - Ⓑ got rid of
   - Ⓒ cleaned
   - Ⓓ painted

3. Most of the men had <u>frostbite</u>.
   - Ⓐ warm winter clothing
   - Ⓑ trouble breathing
   - Ⓒ frozen body parts
   - Ⓓ teeth problems

4. The <u>floes</u> floated out toward the open sea.
   - Ⓐ sheets of ice
   - Ⓑ Antarctic plants
   - Ⓒ boats
   - Ⓓ men

5. The men struggled through a <u>raging</u> storm.
   - Ⓐ winter
   - Ⓑ ocean
   - Ⓒ very strong
   - Ⓓ summer

6. The men who stayed behind were <u>apprehensive</u>.
   - Ⓐ happy
   - Ⓑ worried
   - Ⓒ sorry
   - Ⓓ hungry

7. Shackleton always helped others by his <u>toil</u>.
   - Ⓐ quick mind
   - Ⓑ kindness
   - Ⓒ money
   - Ⓓ hard work

8. Their arms <u>ached</u> from rowing all day.
   - Ⓐ felt stronger
   - Ⓑ stretched
   - Ⓒ hurt
   - Ⓓ smelled

LESSON 12

Division— Writing About Parts

SELECTION DETAILS

Summary

"Separation of Powers" (page 75): This article discusses the three branches of the U.S. government.

"Food Chains and Food Webs" (page 77): This article identifies the three key parts of a food chain or food web: producers, consumers, and decomposers.

Selection Type

Social Studies Article
Science Article

Comprehension Skill

Identify Structural Patterns Found in Nonfiction

Standards

Reading
- Identify structural patterns found in nonfiction.
- Identify details in a reading selection.

Social Studies
- Learn the basic ideas set forth in the Declaration of Independence, Constitution, and Bill of Rights.

Science
- Categorize organisms according to their roles in food chains and webs.

VOCABULARY

Introduce the vocabulary words for each article. Write the words on the board. Help students find a definition for each word. Have students use each word in a sentence.

"Separation of Powers"

principle	Enlightenment
legislative	executive
judicial	

"Food Chains and Food Webs"

producers	herbivores
consumers	omnivores
carnivores	food web
decomposers	photosynthesis

Tap Prior Knowledge

"Separation of Powers": Ask the students if they know what the three branches, or parts, of the U.S. government are. What does each branch do?

"Food Chains and Food Webs": Ask the students if they know what a food chain is. Are they in a food chain? What part of the food chain are they?

Skill to Emphasize

Review the section about division on page 66. Tell the students that division is a kind of writing that tells about the parts of something. A good division article helps the students to see more easily how the parts work together to make up the object.

Preview Text Features

Point out the title of each article. The titles give the students information about the things that will be divided. Have the students look at the illustrations. The illustrations show the parts that make up the whole. Boldfaced words indicate vocabulary words.

Comprehending the Selection

Model a better understanding of division by asking: *What are the parts that make up the whole?*

Reinforce the Comprehension Skill

Tell the students that a good division article helps them to see how the parts of an object go together to form the whole object. Each part is important and necessary to make the whole. Without producers, for example, the consumers would have nothing to eat.

Assess

Have the students complete the activities for each selection.

Have the students write about something they know that has several parts. Have them identify the whole object, and then identify and describe the parts that make up the whole.

Have the students look for instruction manuals that show all the parts of a machine. Have them bring the manuals to school to share with the class.

Separation of Powers

The fourth **principle** of the Constitution is the separation of powers. This means the powers of the government are divided among three branches of government. Dividing power prevents one part of the government from becoming too powerful. Montesquieu, a well-known French thinker during the **Enlightenment**, developed the idea of the three branches of government. The **legislative** branch is led by Congress, which makes laws. The **executive** branch carries out the laws passed by Congress. The executive branch is led by the President and the Vice President. The **judicial** branch of the government includes the federal court system. The Supreme Court is the nation's highest court.

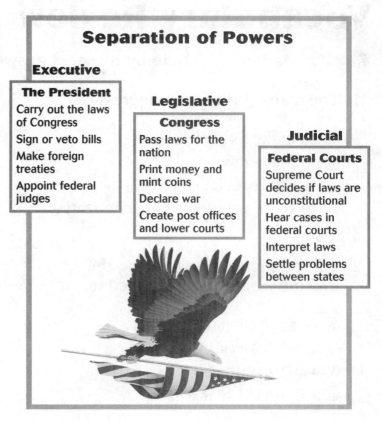

Separation of Powers

Executive

The President
Carry out the laws of Congress
Sign or veto bills
Make foreign treaties
Appoint federal judges

Legislative

Congress
Pass laws for the nation
Print money and mint coins
Declare war
Create post offices and lower courts

Judicial

Federal Courts
Supreme Court decides if laws are unconstitutional
Hear cases in federal courts
Interpret laws
Settle problems between states

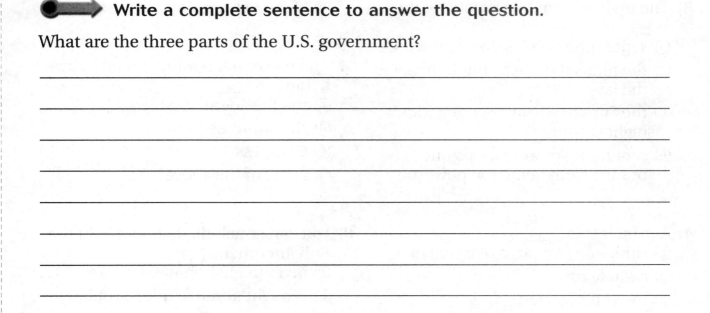

Write a complete sentence to answer the question.

What are the three parts of the U.S. government?

_____

_____

_____

_____

_____

_____

_____

_____

_____

Comprehension and Vocabulary Review

→ **Darken the circle by the best answer.**

1. The main purpose of Congress is
   ____.
   Ⓐ to make foreign treaties
   Ⓑ to make laws
   Ⓒ to interpret laws
   Ⓓ to settle problems between states

2. After Congress passes a law, the
   executive branch is supposed to
   ____.
   Ⓐ change the law
   Ⓑ ask for money
   Ⓒ carry out the law
   Ⓓ interpret the law

3. The main idea of this article is that
   ____.
   Ⓐ separating powers does not work
   Ⓑ the judicial branch should make
      the laws
   Ⓒ the Supreme Court is the nation's
      highest court
   Ⓓ separating powers keeps one
      branch from being too powerful

4. A principle is ____.
   Ⓐ someone in charge of a school
   Ⓑ a guideline
   Ⓒ the son of a king
   Ⓓ something that is easy to do

5. You can conclude from the article
   that the writers of the Constitution
   ____.
   Ⓐ wanted to balance the powers in
      government
   Ⓑ did not know much about
      government
   Ⓒ really wanted to have four
      branches of government
   Ⓓ had some bad ideas

6. The power to declare war belongs to
   ____.
   Ⓐ the President
   Ⓑ the Supreme Court
   Ⓒ Congress
   Ⓓ None of the above

7. The power to appoint federal judges
   belongs to ____.
   Ⓐ the President
   Ⓑ the Supreme Court
   Ⓒ Congress
   Ⓓ None of the above

8. You can conclude that people in the
   Enlightenment ____.
   Ⓐ invented light bulbs
   Ⓑ thought about serious problems
   Ⓒ spent a lot of time outdoors
   Ⓓ did not weigh much

Food Chains and Food Webs

Like the pieces of a puzzle, all living things have a special place in nature. In that place, they find the resources they need to live. One important resource for life is food. You know that plants, from the smallest moss to the largest redwood tree, use resources where they live to make their own food. Animals depend on these plants and other animals as food resources. All living things are connected by their need for food. The simplest connections are called food chains.

Food chains begin with the Sun's energy and **producers**. Producers are usually green plants that make their own food through **photosynthesis**. All the other creatures in the food chain are called **consumers**. Consumers that eat only plants are called **herbivores**. Consumers that eat only animals are called **carnivores**. And consumers that eat both plants and animals are called **omnivores**.

Imagine a simple food chain. A huge oak tree captures the Sun's energy and makes food to live. A rabbit eats the acorn that falls from the oak tree. A hawk eats the rabbit. No other animal eats the hawk. It dies by sickness, accident, or age, and completes one food chain. Once the hawk dies, though, a new food chain begins. The hawk is eaten by a vulture, a bird that feeds on dead animals. Then, **decomposers** such as bacteria or fungi return the hawk's remains to the soil for new producers.

But food chains aren't always so simple. Living things can belong to different food chains at the same time. Several food chains form a **food web**, a collection of chains that cross each other. Each food chain and food web, though, must have three parts: producers, consumers, and decomposers. These three parts are always connected in their search for food.

Food Chains and Food Webs

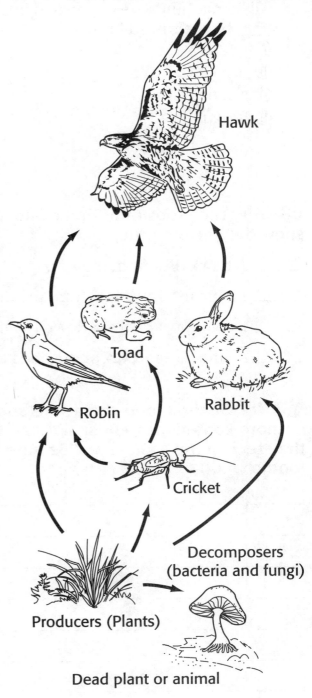

This is a simple food web. A real food web includes many, many more kinds of consumers.

Nonfiction Comprehension: Grades 5–6, SV 8948-6

Name _____ Date_____

Comprehension Review

 Darken the circle by the best answer.

1. All living things are connected in a ____ by their need for food.
   Ⓐ puzzle
   Ⓑ food chain
   Ⓒ sickness
   Ⓓ fungus

2. The main idea of this article is that ____.
   Ⓐ carnivores eat meat
   Ⓑ some consumers eat both plants and meat
   Ⓒ living things depend on other living things for food
   Ⓓ no other animal eats a hawk

 The steps of a food chain are listed below. Write 1, 2, 3, and 4 to show the correct order.

_____ A hawk dies from old age.

_____ Plants use nutrients from the dead hawk to grow.

_____ Decomposers break down the hawk's remains.

_____ A vulture eats part of the dead hawk.

 Several food chains are shown in the diagram on page 77. Write one or more sentences to describe one food chain shown in the diagram. Explain the steps in the food chain. Be sure to include the three major parts of the food chain.

_____

_____

_____

_____

_____

_____

_____

Nonfiction Comprehension: Grades 5–6, SV 8948-6

Name _____ Date_____

Vocabulary Review

 Darken the circle by the best answer.

1. Plants called _____ use the Sun's energy to make food.
   - Ⓐ producers
   - Ⓑ consumers
   - Ⓒ decomposers
   - Ⓓ carnivores

2. All living things that live by eating other living things are _____.
   - Ⓐ producers
   - Ⓑ consumers
   - Ⓒ decomposers
   - Ⓓ photosynthesis

3. Bacteria and fungi that eat dead things are called _____.
   - Ⓐ producers
   - Ⓑ consumers
   - Ⓒ decomposers
   - Ⓓ food webs

4. The process plants use to make food is called _____.
   - Ⓐ photosynthesis
   - Ⓑ food chain
   - Ⓒ food web
   - Ⓓ None of the above

5. Consumers that eat only plants are called _____.
   - Ⓐ herbivores
   - Ⓑ carnivores
   - Ⓒ omnivores
   - Ⓓ decomposers

6. Animals that eat only other animals are called _____.
   - Ⓐ herbivores
   - Ⓑ carnivores
   - Ⓒ omnivores
   - Ⓓ decomposers

7. Consumers that eat both plants and animals are called _____.
   - Ⓐ herbivores
   - Ⓑ carnivores
   - Ⓒ omnivores
   - Ⓓ decomposers

8. Several food chains combine to form a _____.
   - Ⓐ photosynthesis
   - Ⓑ food web
   - Ⓒ food market
   - Ⓓ None of the above

Nonfiction Comprehension: Grades 5–6, SV 8948-6

UNIT 5 Classification

Classification is concerned with the relationship between a thing and others of its kind. Formal classification is used to classify things, or to place them in groups. This grouping is based on similarities of the things being grouped. Comparison-contrast is used to show the similarities and differences between two things. In both these forms, classification is used to show how one thing is related to other similar things. The details of similarity and contrast are provided by description.

• Classification (Lesson 13)

Students are involved with classification on a daily basis. They are grouped according to their gender, their school grade, and their family associations. They watch TV shows grouped by kind, study groups of subjects in school, and play different kinds of sports. Classification is a skill that students learn early in their school life. They may be asked to group shapes according to color or size, for example. They may be asked to identify their favorite food or color.

The process of classification moves from general to specific. A tree diagram is helpful for illustrating this concept; one is provided on page 122. The first level of classification is a very general group, such as Fruits. The next level of classification is more specific. The names of specific fruits are added to the diagram, such as apples, oranges, bananas, and grapes. Then, very specific descriptive details about each fruit are added to the diagram. These details can be used later for comparison-contrast of two fruits.

A tree diagram can have many levels, depending on the needs of the classification. For example, the classification of Fruits could add extra levels. Instead of naming only fruits under the general heading, one could add extra subheadings of kinds of fruits, such as Citrus Fruits and Tropical Fruits. Then, specific fruits could be added to these subheadings, and specific details could be provided for each fruit.

To identify the groups in a classification:
- Use the Classification Tree Diagram on page 122.
- First identify the general group (for example, kinds of pets).
- Then identify any subgroups under the general group (for example, kinds of dogs).
- Then identify the specific members of the general group or subgroup.
- Identify the specific details about each member.
- Think about why the specific members belong in the general group.

You might want to distribute a tree diagram and allow the students to perform a classification before reading the selections. A common topic such as Snacks or Sports would be a good place to start.

• Comparison-Contrast (Lesson 14)

Students can easily relate to the concept of comparison-contrast by introducing it using the terms *alike* and *different*. How are two games alike? How are they different? However, comparison-contrast works well only if the two items are from a common category. For example, comparing and contrasting two kinds of food is logical. Comparing and contrasting a banana and a brick is not really logical.

Comparison-contrast is used to show the similarities and differences between things. *Compare* means to show how things are alike. *Contrast* means to show how things are different. If possible, a comparison-contrast should be limited to two items. Three points of comparison-contrast should be used. For example, two people could be compared and contrasted based on their height, weight, and shoe size. The details about group members in a Tree Diagram are useful in comparing and contrasting.

A Venn Diagram is a useful tool for comparing and contrasting. A Venn Diagram is provided on page 123. The Venn Diagram graphically represents the similarities and differences. The differences are placed in the outer parts of the ovals. The similarities are placed where the two ovals intersect. You might want to distribute a Venn Diagram and allow the students to perform a comparison-contrast before reading the selections. A simple comparison-contrast of apples and oranges would be a good starting point.

To get the most information from a comparison-contrast:
- Use the Venn Diagram on page 123.
- First identify the two things being compared and contrasted.
- Then identify the points used to compare and contrast the two things.
- Think about the ways the things are alike and different.
- Often, the writer is trying to show that one thing is better than another. So be aware of any attempt to persuade the reader.

• Graphic Organizers

Classification Tree Diagram	page 122
Venn Diagram	page 123

LESSON 13

SELECTION DETAILS

Summary
"Kinds of Germs" (page 82): This article classifies four kinds of germs that can cause disease.

"How Stars Are Classified" (page 84): This article discusses the ways scientists classify stars.

"Three Kinds of Resources" (page 86): This article classifies three resources involved in economics.

Selection Type
Science Articles
Social Studies Article

Comprehension Skill
Identify Classification in a Nonfiction Article

Standards
Reading
- Use reading strategies (classification) to comprehend text.
- Identify structural patterns found in nonfiction.
- Identify details in selection.

Science
- Arrange several organisms into a classification system.
- Understand the structure and dynamics of objects in space.

Economics
- Describe the characteristics of production and exchange in an economy.

VOCABULARY

Introduce the vocabulary words for each article. Help students find a definition for each word. Have students use each word in a sentence.

"Kinds of Germs"
disease, bacteria, protozoa, fungi, viruses, reproduce

"How Stars Are Classified"
astronomers, brightness

"Three Kinds of Resources"
economics, resources, natural resources, raw materials, conservation of resources, human resources, capital resources

Classification

BEFORE READING

Tap Prior Knowledge
"Kinds of Germs": Ask the students if they have ever been sick. Ask them what caused their disease.

"How Stars Are Classified": Ask the students if they have looked up at the stars in the sky. Are the stars near or far? Are they large or small? How would the students classify stars?

"Three Kinds of Resources": Ask the students to name one thing they brought to school that day. Where did it come from? How did they get it?

Skill to Emphasize
Review the section about classification on page 80. Tell the students that writers often put things in groups to help the reader to identify them more easily.

DURING READING

Preview Text Features
Have the students look at the illustrations in the "Kinds of Germs" article. Then help the students to envision the four kinds of germs. Have the students look at the chart in "How Stars Are Classified." The chart shows the classification system used by scientists. Boldfaced words indicate vocabulary words.

Comprehending the Selection
Model a better understanding of classification by asking: *What general group of things is being discussed? What are the individual members of that group?*

AFTER READING

Reinforce the Comprehension Skill
Tell the students that a good classification helps them to understand the common features between groups of things. Ask the students to point out the members of each group named in the title of the article. Distribute copies of the Classification Tree Diagram on page 122 to help the students organize the information.

Assess
Have the students complete the activities for each selection.

WRITE ABOUT IT

Distribute copies of the Classification Tree Diagram on page 122. Have the students choose a general group to classify. Have them include at least three individual members of that group. They should also include details about each individual member. Then, have them write a short classification essay using the information they have compiled in their tree diagram.

AT HOME

Have students look in the newspaper or news magazines for articles that contain classification. Have them bring the articles to school to share with the class.

Nonfiction Comprehension: Grades 5–6, SV 8948-6

Name _____ Date _____

Kinds of Germs

Disease is a sickness in your body. It can be caused by many different kinds of germs that work in different ways. Your immune system works to protect you from germs and disease.

Bacteria are one-celled living things. Many kinds of bacteria are important in nature. Some work as decomposers, returning dead plant and animal material to the soil for living things to use. But other bacteria can cause disease. Once these bacteria enter your body, they act in different ways. For example, some bacteria kill healthy body cells. Others make poisons that are carried in your blood to other parts of your body.

Protozoa are also one-celled living things. They feed on other living things. Protozoa are grouped by the ways in which they move. Some have tails that work like whips. Others have tiny hairs that work like oars on a boat. And others can change their body shapes to move. Living things like mosquitoes carry protozoa. The mosquito bites, and protozoa move from the mosquito into the bloodstream of the victim.

Fungi can be made of just one cell, or they may be made of many cells. Like bacteria, fungi are important decomposers. People also use them to make medicines and food. But some fungi can cause disease. Poisons from fungi like molds and mushrooms can enter the bloodstream and cause dangerous or even deadly results.

Viruses are small and cause disease, too. But they are not living things. They depend on living cells to help them **reproduce**. Viruses enter certain cells, reproduce, and then kill the cells as the new viruses spill into the blood.

Four Different Germs

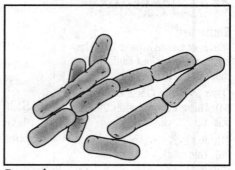
Bacteria

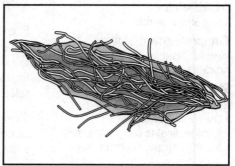
Protozoa

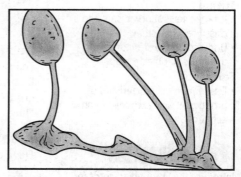
Fungi

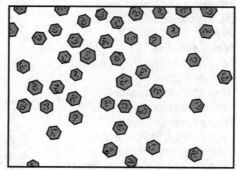
Viruses

Lesson 13: Classification
Nonfiction Comprehension: Grades 5–6, SV 8948-6

Comprehension and Vocabulary Review

 Darken the circle by the best answer.

1. Bacteria are ____.
   - Ⓐ one-celled dead things
   - Ⓑ two-celled dead things
   - Ⓒ one-celled living things
   - Ⓓ two-celled living things

2. After viruses enter certain cells, they ____.
   - Ⓐ explode
   - Ⓑ reproduce
   - Ⓒ eat the cells
   - Ⓓ make poison

3. Bacteria, protozoa, fungi, and viruses are grouped together because they are all ____.
   - Ⓐ worms
   - Ⓑ germs
   - Ⓒ living things
   - Ⓓ funny looking

4. According to the article, protozoa can enter your body through ____.
   - Ⓐ decomposers
   - Ⓑ medicines
   - Ⓒ fungi
   - Ⓓ an insect's bite

 Write complete sentences to answer the questions.

5. Scientists classify things. What are the four kinds of germs discussed in the article?

   _____

   _____

6. Which kind of germ includes some molds and mushrooms?

   _____

   _____

7. You can classify things, too. What are four diseases that might be caused by germs?

   _____

   _____

Nonfiction Comprehension: Grades 5–6, SV 8948-6

How Stars Are Classified

The light from a candle can be bright. The light from a street lamp burning outside your window can be dim. The candle's light seems brighter because the candle is closer to you. When you see a star in the sky that is brighter than the stars around it, it may just be closer to Earth. The bright star may even be much smaller and much cooler than other stars you see, but because it's closer to you, it seems brighter.

There are important differences among stars. Some are so huge, they're called supergiants. Others are smaller than Earth. Some are very hot and bright, while others are cooler and dim. Stars also have colors, from the hottest blue stars to the coolest red stars. **Astronomers** use these differences to group, or classify, stars. Classifying stars helps astronomers explain how stars form, how they change, and how they die.

There are two ways astronomers classify the **brightness** of stars. The first way classifies stars by how bright they appear when they are seen from Earth. But stars that are closer to Earth often seem brighter, so the second way to classify stars is by how bright the stars really are. Astronomers determine how bright stars would be if they were all the same distance from Earth. Then, they give each star a number based on its brightness. Very bright stars have low numbers. Dim stars have high numbers.

Astronomers also classify stars by their colors. Stars with very hot outer layers appear blue. Cooler stars appear red. Stars like the Sun are medium-hot stars. They are yellow. To classify stars by temperature and color, astronomers use one of the letters on the scale O, B, A, F, G, K, and M. The letter *O* goes to the hottest stars. The letter *M* goes to the coolest stars. The Sun has the letter *G*. It is a star with average brightness and temperature.

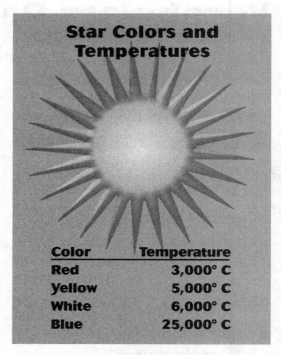

Star Colors and Temperatures

Color	Temperature
Red	3,000° C
Yellow	5,000° C
White	6,000° C
Blue	25,000° C

The hottest stars, which give off a blue color, have an average surface temperature of 25,000° C. The coolest stars, which give off a red color, have an average surface temperature of 3,000° C.

Name _____ Date _____

Comprehension and Vocabulary Review

→ **Darken the circle by the best answer.**

1. An astronomer is a person who studies ____.
   Ⓐ storms
   Ⓑ names
   Ⓒ stars
   Ⓓ trains

2. Astronomers classify stars according to color and ____.
   Ⓐ brightness
   Ⓑ shape
   Ⓒ distance
   Ⓓ smell

3. Blue stars are the ____.
   Ⓐ hottest
   Ⓑ coolest
   Ⓒ brightest
   Ⓓ smallest

4. Red stars are the ____.
   Ⓐ hottest
   Ⓑ coolest
   Ⓒ brightest
   Ⓓ None of the above

5. Stars given the letter *O* are the ____ stars.
   Ⓐ hottest
   Ⓑ coolest
   Ⓒ smallest
   Ⓓ oldest

6. The Sun is a star of average brightness and ____.
   Ⓐ color
   Ⓑ distance
   Ⓒ size
   Ⓓ temperature

→ **Write complete sentences to answer the question. Use another sheet of paper if necessary.**

7. What do you think would happen to life on Earth if the Sun was an O star?

   _____

   _____

   _____

   _____

   _____

   _____

Nonfiction Comprehension: Grades 5–6, SV 8948-6

Three Kinds of Resources

Economics is about the use and transfer of **resources**. **Natural resources** are one kind of resource. Natural resources are things that occur in nature. Land, rocks, and water are a few natural resources. So are iron, coal, and oil. Plants and animals are natural resources, too. But buildings, streets, and cars are not natural resources. People do not make natural resources. People use natural resources to make things. Sometimes, natural resources are called **raw materials**. From these raw materials, people make finished products.

Our natural resources should not be wasted or destroyed. **Conservation of resources** means to manage and use our resources wisely. Laws have been passed so that people do not waste our precious resources. Many things are made from natural resources. If natural resources are wasted, not as many things can be made. Then, the cost of those things will increase. If we do not conserve resources, we will have to pay more for the things we want to buy.

Human resources are another kind of resource. Human resources are the people who do labor. They work in many different kinds of jobs. They may make things, or they may help other people. Your teacher is a human resource. So are clerks, cowboys, and carpenters. Anyone who works is a human resource. A machine is not a human resource.

Capital resources are a third kind of resource. Capital resources are made by people. They are used by people to make other things. They may also be used to do work or to provide a service. Workers in factories use machines to make clothes. Farmers use tractors to plow their land to grow crops. Plumbers use special tools to repair broken pipes. Machines, tractors, and tools are capital resources. The factory building is a capital resource, too. Most capital resources are made from natural resources.

Comprehension and Vocabulary Review

➡ **Darken the circle by the best answer.**

1. Economics deals with the use and transfer of ____.
   Ⓐ economies
   Ⓑ resources
   Ⓒ broken pipes
   Ⓓ pollution

2. ____ are things that occur in nature.
   Ⓐ Natural resources
   Ⓑ Conservation of resources
   Ⓒ Human resources
   Ⓓ Capital resources

3. People use ____ to make finished products.
   Ⓐ economics
   Ⓑ raw materials
   Ⓒ conservation
   Ⓓ None of the above

4. ____ are the people who do labor.
   Ⓐ Natural resources
   Ⓑ Conservation of resources
   Ⓒ Human resources
   Ⓓ Capital resources

5. A synonym for *labor* is ____.
   Ⓐ laboratory
   Ⓑ play
   Ⓒ sleeping
   Ⓓ work

6. According to the article, ____ are made by people.
   Ⓐ natural resources
   Ⓑ conservation of resources
   Ⓒ human resources
   Ⓓ capital resources

➡ **Write complete sentences to answer the question. Use another sheet of paper if necessary.**

7. Why do you think it is important to conserve natural resources?

_____

_____

_____

_____

_____

_____

What Kind of Resource?

Production makes use of all the resources. The human resources are the workers. The workers use natural resources, or raw materials, to make a product. The workers also use capital resources, or equipment, to help them to make the product.

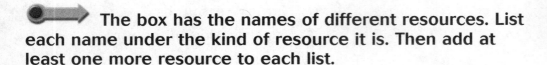 The box has the names of different resources. List each name under the kind of resource it is. Then add at least one more resource to each list.

camera	fish	farmland	designer	teacher
water	paint store	oil	janitor	desk
computer	trees	telephone	letter carrier	carpenter

Natural Resources	Human Resources	Capital Resources
_____	_____	_____
_____	_____	_____
_____	_____	_____
_____	_____	_____
_____	_____	_____
_____	_____	_____
_____	_____	_____
_____	_____	_____
_____	_____	_____
_____	_____	_____
_____	_____	_____

Comparison-Contrast

Summary
"Renewable and Nonrenewable Resources" (page 90) compares and contrasts these two kinds of resources.

"Federalism" (page 91) compares and contrasts the powers delegated to or shared by the federal and state governments.

"Electric Circuits" (page 93) compares and contrasts series and parallel circuits.

"Apes" (page 95) compares and contrasts four kinds of apes.

Selection Type
Science Articles
Social Studies Articles

Comprehension Skill
Identify Comparison-Contrast in a Nonfiction Article

Standards
Reading
- Understand the use of comparison and contrast in a nonfiction selection.
- Identify details in a selection.

Science
- Identify renewable and nonrenewable resources.
- Understand that energy moves in predictable ways.
- Based on attributes, place living organisms into groups based on similarities.

Social Studies
- Learn the basic ideas set forth in the Declaration of Independence, Constitution, and Bill of Rights.

VOCABULARY

"Renewable and Nonrenewable Resources"
renewable, nonrenewable
"Federalism"
federalism, delegates
"Electric Circuits"
circuit, series circuit, interrupted, parallel circuit
"Apes"
primates, gorillas, gibbons, ferocious, chimpanzees, orangutans

BEFORE READING

Tap Prior Knowledge
"Renewable and Nonrenewable Resources": Ask the students if they know the difference between these two kinds of resources. Why might it be a good idea to conserve nonrenewable resources?

"Federalism": Ask the students if they know what kinds of things the federal government can do that state governments cannot do, and vice versa.

"Electric Circuits": Ask the students if they know the difference between a series circuit and a parallel circuit. Which do they think might be better for a string of lights?

"Apes": Ask the students what they know about the four kinds of apes discussed in this article. Is any kind similar to humans?

Skill to Emphasize
Review the section about comparison-contrast on page 80. Tell the students that *compare* means to show how things are alike and *contrast* means to show how things are different.

Preview Text Features
Point out the chart in "Federalism." It gives information about the powers that the federal and state governments have. The diagrams in "Electric Circuits" show how each kind of circuit is arranged. The illustrations in "Apes" help the students to envision the four kinds of apes being discussed. Boldfaced words indicate vocabulary words.

Comprehending the Selection
Model a better understanding of comparison-contrast by asking: *In what ways are the two things alike and different?*

Reinforce the Comprehension Skill
Tell the students that comparison-contrast helps them to understand how two things are alike and different. The two things are of the same general group, so they have basic common features. The differences are what allow the students to tell one thing from the other. Distribute copies of the Venn diagram on page 123 to help the students organize the information.

Assess
Have the students complete the activities for each selection.

Renewable and Nonrenewable Resources

The resources that people use on Earth can be divided into two different groups: **renewable** and **nonrenewable**. Nature provides people with renewable resources. Air, water, and all living things, including animals and food plants, are renewable resources. There will always be more of these resources, as long as people use them carefully.

Nonrenewable resources are those resources that Earth made long ago. They cannot be made again, except over a very long period of time. These resources were once the remains of plant and animal life. Over a period of millions of years, heat and pressure deep inside Earth turned these remains into oil, coal, gas, and different kinds of metals. Many of these nonrenewable resources are important because they can be used as fuel.

➡️ **Write a complete sentence to answer each question.**

1. How are renewable and nonrenewable resources alike?

_____

_____

_____

2. How are renewable and nonrenewable resources different?

_____

_____

_____

3. Why are many nonrenewable resources important?

_____

_____

Nonfiction Comprehension: Grades 5–6, SV 8948-6

Federalism

The second principle of the U.S. Constitution is **federalism**. This means power is shared between the state governments and the federal, or central, government. This is shown in the diagram below. For example, both state governments and the federal government can collect taxes. Though power is shared, each government also has certain powers that the other does not. Only the federal government can print money, but only the state governments can control business within the state.

If power is shared, what happens when federal and state laws disagree? The **delegates** decided that the Constitution is the nation's highest law. So all federal and state laws must obey the Constitution. Likewise, all federal laws must be obeyed over state laws.

Federalism: Shared Powers

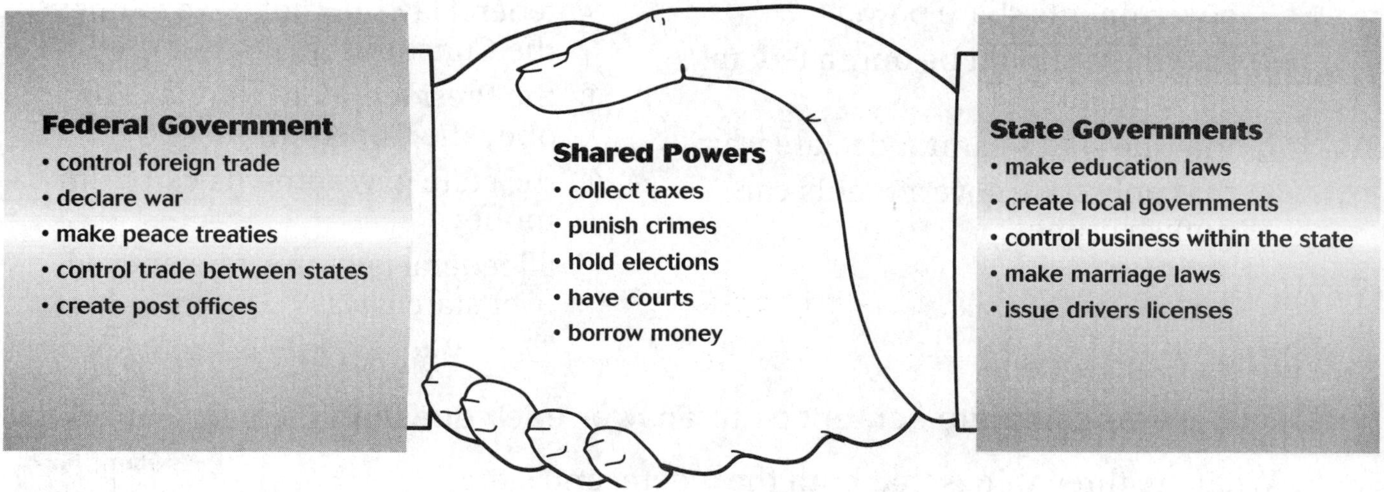

Federal Government
- control foreign trade
- declare war
- make peace treaties
- control trade between states
- create post offices

Shared Powers
- collect taxes
- punish crimes
- hold elections
- have courts
- borrow money

State Governments
- make education laws
- create local governments
- control business within the state
- make marriage laws
- issue drivers licenses

Name _____ **Date** _____

Comprehension and Vocabulary Review

 Darken the circle by the best answer.

1. A delegate is ____.
   - Ⓐ a place to buy lunch meat
   - Ⓑ a representative at a convention
   - Ⓒ a special kind of gate
   - Ⓓ a judge

2. The main idea of federalism is ____.
   - Ⓐ that the federal and state governments share power
   - Ⓑ that there should be only a federal government
   - Ⓒ that the states cannot declare war
   - Ⓓ that only state governments can punish crimes

3. According to the article, all federal and state laws must obey ____.
   - Ⓐ the President
   - Ⓑ the Supreme Court
   - Ⓒ the Constitution
   - Ⓓ the state governments

4. According to the article, ____.
   - Ⓐ federal laws do not have to obey the Constitution
   - Ⓑ the President does not have to obey the Constitution
   - Ⓒ the state governments can print money
   - Ⓓ all federal laws must be obeyed over state laws

Write complete sentences to answer each question.

5. What are three things that both the federal and state governments can do?

   _____

   _____

6. What are three things that the federal government can do but state governments cannot do?

   _____

   _____

7. What are three things that state governments can do but the federal government cannot do?

   _____

   _____

Nonfiction Comprehension: Grades 5–6, SV 8948-6

Electric Circuits

We depend on a steady flow of electric current to power our lights and machines. This steady flow moves through a complete loop, or electric **circuit**. An electric circuit can be as small as the circuit inside a flashlight, or as large as the circuit that supplies electricity to a town or city. An electric circuit needs a push, or force, to keep the current moving. The strength of this force determines how much energy the current carries. The power plant produces a greater force than the small battery in a flashlight.

In a **series circuit**, objects such as light bulbs are connected in one large loop. If any part of the circuit is broken, the electric current cannot complete its movement. Let's use a string of holiday lights to explain why this might be a problem. One wire is connected to a battery. The same wire connects each light in the string. The wire completes the circuit when it's joined to the opposite end of the battery. If the wire in one bulb on the string breaks, the circuit is broken. The current is **interrupted**, and the other lights on the string will not work.

If the string of holiday lights uses a **parallel circuit**, each light in the string is connected to the battery in a complete circuit. Think of the string of lights as a ladder. Each bulb sits in the middle of one rung. Electric current moves from the battery up one side of the ladder, across the rung to the other side of the ladder, and back to the battery. If one of the rungs, or lights, breaks, the other lights still work.

In a series circuit, all the light bulbs share the total amount of electricity. If you add extra bulbs, each light receives less electricity, and the lights become dimmer. In a parallel circuit, each bulb receives the same amount of electricity. Adding extra bulbs does not change the brightness of the bulbs.

A Simple Electric Circuit

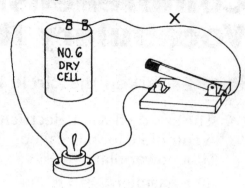

A Series Circuit

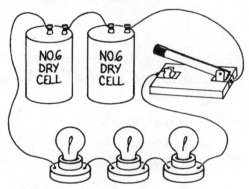

If one part of the circuit burns out or breaks, the current flow stops in the circuit.

A Parallel Circuit

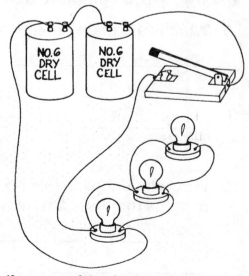

If one part of the circuit burns out or breaks, the current still flows in the rest of the circuit.

Name _____ Date _____

Comprehension and Vocabulary Review

⬤➡ **Darken the circle by the best answer.**

1. The steady flow of electricity through a complete loop is called ____.
   - Ⓐ a power plant
   - Ⓑ a flashlight
   - Ⓒ an electric circuit
   - Ⓓ a light bulb

2. In a ____, things in the circuit are connected in one line or loop.
   - Ⓐ series circuit
   - Ⓑ parallel circuit
   - Ⓒ current
   - Ⓓ ladder

3. If a light burns out in a parallel circuit, ____.
   - Ⓐ all the lights will go out
   - Ⓑ all the lights will explode
   - Ⓒ the other lights will not go out
   - Ⓓ the other lights will get dimmer

4. If a light burns out in a series circuit, ____.
   - Ⓐ all the lights will go out
   - Ⓑ all the lights will explode
   - Ⓒ the other lights will not go out
   - Ⓓ the other lights will get dimmer

⬤➡ **Write complete sentences to answer each question.**

5. What is the main difference between a series circuit and a parallel circuit?

   _____

   _____

   _____

6. Why would it probably take more time to replace a burned-out bulb in a string of lights that uses a series circuit than in one that uses a parallel circuit?

   _____

   _____

   _____

Apes

Apes belong to a group of mammals called **primates**. Primates include monkeys, apes, and humans. There are four kinds of apes. They are gibbons, chimpanzees, orangutans, and gorillas.

Gibbons are the smallest apes. They usually live in pairs in the high mountain forests of Asia. Gibbons use their long arms to swing from tree to tree. They feed on leaves and fruit. They often walk on two legs along the tree branches as they feed.

Chimpanzees live together in small groups in Africa. Chimpanzees are very good climbers but also spend time on the ground. They eat fruit and other parts of plants. Wild chimpanzees sometimes use tools. For example, a chimpanzee may use a twig to gather insects to eat.

Orangutans are bigger than chimpanzees. They can be found in some forests of Asia. Orangutans live by themselves. They make nests out of branches and leaves to sleep in each night. During the day, they climb through trees, looking for fruit to eat.

Gorillas are the largest apes. They live in small groups in the forests of Africa. Gorillas eat grass, leaves, and fruit. They spend most of their time on the ground. At night, the females and young may sleep in tree nests. But tree branches may not be strong enough to hold large male gorillas. So they sleep on the ground. Gorillas look **ferocious**. But they are actually shy, friendly animals.

Gibbon

Chimpanzee

Orangutan

Gorilla

Nonfiction Comprehension: Grades 5–6, SV 8948-6

Comprehension and Vocabulary Review

➤ Use details from the article to complete each sentence.

1. Apes belong to a group of mammals called _____.

2. Primates include _____, _____, and
_____.

3. The four kinds of apes are _____, _____,
_____, and _____.

➤ Write **gibbons**, **chimpanzees**, **orangutans**, or **gorillas** to answer each question.

4. Which apes live in pairs? _____

5. Which apes live by themselves? _____

6. Which two apes live in groups? _____

7. Which apes are the largest? _____

8. Which apes are the smallest? _____

9. Which apes use tools? _____

10. Which two apes are usually found in Asia? _____
_____

11. Which two apes are usually found in Africa? _____
_____

12. Which apes look ferocious but are actually shy and friendly? _____
_____

Nonfiction Comprehension: Grades 5–6, SV 8948-6

UNIT 6 Conclusion

Sometimes an author may not tell the reader directly what is happening in an article. Sometimes the reader must make a conclusion based on the facts of the article or the reader's own experiences or observations. After making a conclusion, the reader may need to change it if additional facts and details are gathered. Sometimes the reader must also determine the writer's purpose or conclude if a writer's statement is a fact or an opinion.

• Drawing Conclusions (Lesson 15)

A conclusion is a logical judgment based on a set of facts. If there are mud tracks on the carpet, one can logically conclude that the person with mud on his or her shoes made those tracks. New facts may cause the conclusion to be incorrect, but the conclusion is reasonable based on the facts that are available. In drawing conclusions, the reader must pay attention to all the facts. A conclusion is not logical or valid if it is based on only some of the facts; a good conclusion is based on all of the facts.

However, one cannot say that there is only one conclusion for a set of facts. Many conclusions can be drawn from a set of facts, and they can all be reasonable and valid. Only as new facts are gathered do some of the conclusions become invalid.

Students must sometimes also determine a writer's purpose for writing. Personal writing tells something about the writer or how the writer feels about something. Literary writing tells a story or a poem. Persuasive writing tries to make the readers change their minds about some issue. Informative writing tells facts about a topic. The reader must decide which of these purposes the writer has used.

To draw logical conclusions:
- Read the information carefully.
- Think about the facts and your own experiences and observations.
- Decide what all the facts tell you.
- Write a conclusion based on the facts you have available.
- Be sure your conclusion uses all the facts, not just some.
- Change your conclusion if new facts show something different.

• Fact or Opinion? (Lesson 16)

Nonfiction articles contain facts. Nonfiction articles sometimes also give opinions, or a person's beliefs. Facts are used to inform, and opinions are used to persuade. Sometimes a reader must decide, or conclude, if a statement is a fact or an opinion. Writers often use facts to support their opinions. They want to convince the reader that what they are claiming is true. If an article contains opinions, the writer is probably trying to persuade the reader.

Facts can be used to prove an issue. Opinions cannot prove anything. An opinion is simply a person's belief, often not supported by facts of any kind. The opinion is just what that person thinks, right or wrong. Facts are considered always to be right.

How to distinguish facts from opinions:
- Use the Fact-Opinion Chart on page 124.
- Facts can be proven, but opinions cannot be proven.
- When you read a statement, ask yourself, "Can this statement be proven?" If the answer is *yes*, it is a fact. If the answer is *no*, it is an opinion.
- The words *should*, *must*, *think*, and *believe* are often clues that a sentence is an opinion.
- Make a mental note that a statement is a fact or an opinion.
- If you must make a logical conclusion, use only facts, not opinions.

• Graphic Organizers

Fact-Opinion Chart   page 124

Research Base
"Content literacy involves the strategies required to read, comprehend, and write informational texts in a variety of subjects. Different styles and ways of organizing texts are used for different subjects." (*Guiding Readers and Writers: Grades 3–6*, p. 400)

Drawing Conclusions

SELECTION DETAILS

Summary
"Draw a Conclusion" (page 99): The sample paragraphs give practice in drawing conclusions and determining the writer's purpose in short selections.

"Versailles" (page 101): This article briefly describes the Versailles Palace and tells about its construction.

"The End of World War II" (page 103): This article discusses the conditions in the United States during World War II and the events that led to the end of the war.

Selection Type
Social Studies Articles

Comprehension Skill
Draw Conclusions from Facts in a Nonfiction Article

Standards
Reading
• Make and explain inferences from texts such as drawing conclusions.

Social Studies
• Put in chronological order important people and events.
• Examine the relationship between current events and important historical events.

VOCABULARY

Introduce the vocabulary words for each article. Write the words on the board. Help students find a definition for each word. Have students use each word in a sentence.

"Versailles"

monarchy	collosal
mortar	magnificent

"The End of World War II"

Axis	Allies
ambulance	Great Depression
rationed	invaded
D-Day	surrendered
atomic bomb	

BEFORE READING

Tap Prior Knowledge
"Versailles": Ask the students if they have ever seen a palace. What do they think living in a palace might be like?

"The End of World War II": Ask the students if they know anyone who fought in World War II. Have they heard stories or seen movies about the war?

Skill to Emphasize
Review the section about drawing conclusions on page 97. Tell the students that writers sometimes do not tell the reader everything that is happening in an article. The reader sometimes must draw conclusions, or make judgments, about the facts given. The reader at times must also identify the writer's purpose for writing.

DURING READING

Preview Text Features
Have the students look on pages 104 and 105 at the photograph and map in "The End of World War II." The photograph is a famous image from World War II. The map shows the extent of Japanese occupation in the Pacific. Boldfaced words indicate vocabulary words.

Comprehending the Selection
Model a better understanding of conclusion by asking: *Using the facts given, what conclusions can you make about the topic?*

AFTER READING

Reinforce the Comprehension Skill
Tell the students that a good conclusion is based on all the facts of the article. They should be sure their conclusions make sense and include all the facts.

Assess
Have the students complete the activities for each selection.

WRITE ABOUT IT

Have the students write a paragraph telling why they think history is or is not an important thing to know about.

Draw a Conclusion

Read each paragraph and draw a conclusion based on the facts. Darken the circle by the best answer.

Birds were singing. The trees were budding, and tiny flowers peeked up through the brown grass. The Sun was warming the cold ground.

1. It is most likely _____.
   Ⓐ night
   Ⓑ fall
   Ⓒ spring
   Ⓓ summer

Louis Braille invented a simple written language for the blind. Being blind himself, he understood how necessary reading is to a blind person. Now, books, newspapers, and magazines are printed in Braille.

2. Which of the following can be concluded from the passage?
   Ⓐ Louis Braille was also deaf and couldn't speak.
   Ⓑ Braille uses raised dots to make letters.
   Ⓒ The blind can now read books and magazines.
   Ⓓ Louis Braille also invented a Braille typewriter.

Quarrying for rock involves cutting and drilling large enough blocks of rock to use in building. Quarries in Egypt have been providing building rock for 4,500 years. Across the Nile from where the limestone pyramids stand are even older quarries.

3. Which of the following can be concluded from the passage?
   Ⓐ In early quarries, a big problem was moving the rock.
   Ⓑ Crushed rock is very important to road building.
   Ⓒ The pyramids are located in Giza near the Nile River.
   Ⓓ Quarrying for building rock is not a new occupation.

Daniel Boone was born in a wilderness area in Pennsylvania. His family later moved to a desolate area in North Carolina. After cutting the Wilderness Road into Kentucky, Boone moved his wife and his daughter into the area. Later in life, Boone moved still farther west, where he could explore the Rockies.

4. Which of the following can be concluded from the passage?
   Ⓐ Daniel Boone liked living in settled areas.
   Ⓑ Daniel Boone fought in the French and Indian War.
   Ⓒ Daniel Boone learned many of the American Indian ways.
   Ⓓ Boone was always moving west into uncharted areas.

Nonfiction Comprehension: Grades 5–6, SV 8948-6

Name _____ Date _____

Writers have a specific purpose when writing. Personal writing tells something about the writer or how the writer feels about something. Literary writing tells a story or a poem. Persuasive writing tries to make the readers change their minds about some issue. Informative writing tells facts about a topic.

⬤▶ **Read each paragraph and decide the author's purpose in writing. Darken the circle by the best answer.**

The three largest oceans are the Pacific, Atlantic, and Indian Oceans. The Pacific covers about 63,750,000 square miles. The Atlantic covers about 31,830,000 square miles. The Indian Ocean covers about 28,357,000 square miles.

5. What purpose did the writer use for this paragraph?
Ⓐ personal
Ⓑ literary
Ⓒ persuasive
Ⓓ informative

Because of Joseph Lister, many lives have been saved. Lister was an English surgeon who lived about a hundred years ago. Many people died after operations because of infections. Lister learned about the bacteria causing the infections from the work of Louis Pasteur, so he started using antiseptics when he operated. Because antiseptics kill germs, his patients did not get infections. They did not die. It was a great discovery. Everyone should be thankful for the work of Joseph Lister.

6. What purpose did the writer use for this paragraph?
Ⓐ personal
Ⓑ literary
Ⓒ persuasive
Ⓓ informative

The Pueblo Indians of today have as their ancestors the cliff dwellers. They were called cliff dwellers because their homes were built on the side of cliffs. These homes were built over 200 years before Christopher Columbus landed in America. The cliff dwellers were farmers who raised corn and beans. The cliff dwellings were easy to defend against enemies because they were so hard to reach. About 700 years ago, the cliff dwellers left their homes. Some historians believe they left because of a drought, a long period with no rain. No one really knows why these remarkable homes were abandoned.

7. What purpose did the writer use for this paragraph?
Ⓐ personal
Ⓑ literary
Ⓒ persuasive
Ⓓ informative

Versailles

   Almost every visitor to Paris makes a trip to Versailles, the Museum of the **Monarchy.** Versailles was one of the royal palaces of French kings. It gets its name from the city where it was built. When people speak about Versailles, they usually mean the palace, not the city.

   At the rear of the palace is a large courtyard paved with granite blocks. Beyond the courtyard are the avenues of the city. They were cut through the city by King Louis XIV. The avenues are shaded on each side by double rows of linden trees. The courtyard contains many **colossal** marble statues of people and a bronze statue of the great Louis sitting on his horse.

   Louis decided that all the houses in the city of Versailles had to be built of brick. That was because he wanted only the royal residences to be built of stone. If any house happened to be made of stone, the stones had to be painted red with dividing lines of white to make them look like brick and **mortar.**

   Although Versailles Palace had **magnificent** fountains, parks, and gardens, beautiful furniture, and works of art, Louis did not spend much time there. He preferred to live in Paris and only visited Versailles occasionally.

Comprehension and Vocabulary Review

Darken the circle by the best answer.

1. In which country was Louis XIV the king?
   Ⓐ Paris
   Ⓑ Versailles
   Ⓒ France
   Ⓓ Europe

2. When people talk about Versailles, you can conclude they usually mean ____.
   Ⓐ the palace
   Ⓑ the city
   Ⓒ the courtyard
   Ⓓ the king

3. Why didn't Louis XIV allow the people of Versailles to build their houses of stone?
   Ⓐ He thought they would not look splendid enough.
   Ⓑ He wanted to see contrast in the houses.
   Ⓒ He wanted the royal residence to look different.
   Ⓓ He was a cruel king.

4. How can you tell that Louis XIV was probably vain?
   Ⓐ He planted miles of linden trees.
   Ⓑ The gardens and parks at Versailles are magnificent.
   Ⓒ He preferred to live in Paris.
   Ⓓ His statue is different from all the others.

5. What can you conclude about Versailles today?
   Ⓐ It is still a royal residence.
   Ⓑ It is still a major tourist attraction.
   Ⓒ It is situated in Paris.
   Ⓓ The furniture is no longer there.

6. What does the word *colossal* mean?
   Ⓐ statues
   Ⓑ gigantic
   Ⓒ marble
   Ⓓ granite

7. What can you conclude about the avenues?
   Ⓐ They were shady and beautiful.
   Ⓑ They were long and narrow.
   Ⓒ Only kings could use them.
   Ⓓ They had beautiful flower gardens.

8. What purpose do you think the writer used to write this article?
   Ⓐ personal
   Ⓑ literary
   Ⓒ persuasive
   Ⓓ informative

Nonfiction Comprehension: Grades 5–6, SV 8948-6

The End of World War II

The **Axis** countries were fighting to conquer many countries during World War II. In December 1941, the United States began to fight in the war with the **Allies**. Millions of American soldiers went to Europe, Africa, and Asia.

Life in the United States changed during the war. Millions of American men were soldiers in the war. Women also joined the United States Army and Navy. Many worked as nurses and **ambulance** drivers in the war. Millions of other women worked in factories to make the ships, airplanes, guns, tanks, and clothing that the soldiers needed. Because there were so many new jobs, the war ended the **Great Depression**.

American farmers worked hard to grow extra crops. The United States sent food to American and other Allied soldiers who were fighting the war. There was not enough food for people at home to have all they wanted. Some foods were **rationed**. Families could buy only small amounts of some foods, such as meat, sugar, and flour. Many people started gardens and grew food for their families.

Soldiers raise the American flag after winning an important battle on Iwo Jima. Iwo Jima is an island in the Pacific Ocean.

The United States needed metal to make weapons. Many people collected old metal. Old metal was used to make ships, guns, tanks, and bullets for the war.

The United States government was unfair to Japanese Americans during the war. Most Japanese Americans lived in Hawaii, California, and other parts of the West Coast. But soon after Japan bombed Pearl Harbor, the government forced thousands of Japanese Americans to move to special camps. They had to live in small rooms. Guards watched the people in these camps day and night. But many Japanese American men decided they wanted to help the United States win the war. They fought for the United States even though they were not treated fairly. They were brave soldiers.

General Dwight D. Eisenhower led the American army in Europe. In 1944 he became the leader of all the Allied soldiers. Soldiers from Great Britain, France, Canada, the United States, and other countries were fighting for the Allies. General Eisenhower helped all these soldiers work together to fight against the Axis countries.

General Eisenhower led the Allied soldiers against Italy. German soldiers went to Italy to help the Italians fight against the Allies. The Allies fought for many months in Italy. At last, in 1944 Italy surrendered.

Adolf Hitler still ruled France and most of Europe. On June 6, 1944, General Eisenhower **invaded** France with thousands of Allied soldiers. This day was called **D-Day**. After D-Day, more Allied soldiers invaded France. After two months the Allied soldiers captured Paris from the Germans. France soon became a free nation again.

The Germans were losing the war. But Adolf Hitler would not surrender. The Allies attacked Germany. American planes dropped bombs on German cities. The Soviet Union also bombed Germany. Much of Germany was destroyed. Finally, on May 7, 1945, the Germans **surrendered** to the Allies. Europe had peace again.

Thousands of Americans were fighting in Asia at the same time General Eisenhower and his soldiers were fighting in Europe. General Douglas MacArthur led American soldiers in Asia. Japan had captured the Philippines, Guam, and other islands in the Pacific Ocean. General MacArthur said that he would help Guam and the Philippines become free again.

General MacArthur and the American soldiers fought the Japanese on many islands in the Pacific Ocean. Admiral Chester W. Nimitz also led Americans in the Pacific. Slowly American soldiers captured many islands from Japan. The American soldiers returned to Guam and the Philippines. In 1944 Guam and the Philippines became free. Then the United States attacked Japan. The Japanese were losing the war. But they would not surrender.

The United States had a powerful new weapon called the **atomic bomb**. Harry S. Truman had become the President of the United States. He wanted the war to end quickly. Every day more Americans were killed during the war. Japan would not stop fighting. President Truman decided to force Japan to surrender. He decided that an American plane would drop an atomic bomb on a Japanese city.

On August 6, 1945, the United States dropped the first atomic bomb. It destroyed most of the city of Hiroshima. Japan would not surrender. A few days later, Americans dropped an atomic bomb on the city of Nagasaki. These powerful bombs killed thousands of Japanese. On August 14, 1945, Japanese leaders surrendered to the Allies. There was peace in Asia. World War II was finally over.

WORLD WAR II IN THE PACIFIC

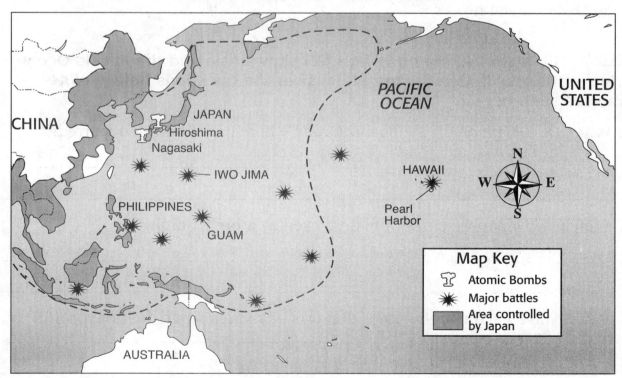

Name _____ Date_____

Comprehension and Vocabulary Review

➤ **Darken the circle by the best answer.**

1. Foods such as sugar, flour, and meat were ____ in the United States during World War II.
   Ⓐ outlawed
   Ⓑ rationed
   Ⓒ not sold
   Ⓓ given away

2. On June 6, 1944, General ____ invaded France with thousands of Allied soldiers.
   Ⓐ Douglas MacArthur
   Ⓑ Chester Nimitz
   Ⓒ Adolf Hitler
   Ⓓ Dwight Eisenhower

3. ____ was President of the United States at the end of World War II.
   Ⓐ Adolf Hitler
   Ⓑ Harry Truman
   Ⓒ Chester Nimitz
   Ⓓ Dwight Eisenhower

4. What purpose do you think the writer used to write this article?
   Ⓐ personal
   Ⓑ literary
   Ⓒ persuasive
   Ⓓ informative

➤ **The historical map on page 105 shows Asia and the Pacific Ocean during World War II. Use the map to answer the questions below. Write complete sentences.**

5. What are two places in the Pacific Ocean where major battles occurred?

   _____

   _____

6. Which two Japanese cities were destroyed by atomic bombs?

   _____

   _____

7. Where did a Pacific battle occur that was in an area Japan did not control?

   _____

   _____

Nonfiction Comprehension: Grades 5–6, SV 8948-6

Drawing Conclusions

➡️ **Read each pair of sentences. Then look in the box for the conclusion you can make. Write the letter of the conclusion on the line.**

> **a.** The United States dropped a second atomic bomb on Japan.
>
> **b.** Some foods were rationed during the war.
>
> **c.** The United States government was unfair to Japanese Americans.
>
> **d.** Many women worked in factories in the United States.
>
> **e.** The Germans surrendered.

1. During the war, millions of American men were in the United States Army. The factories needed workers to make airplanes and weapons.

   Conclusion _____

2. Japanese Americans were forced to move to special camps. Guards watched the people in the camps all the time.

   Conclusion _____

3. The Allies attacked Germany. Much of Germany was destroyed.

   Conclusion _____

4. The United States dropped the first atomic bomb on a city in Japan. Japan still would not surrender.

   Conclusion _____

5. The United States sent food to American soldiers fighting the war. There was not enough food for people at home to have all they wanted.

   Conclusion _____

LESSON 16

SELECTION DETAILS

Summary
"Fact or Opinion?" (page 109): The sample paragraphs give practice in identifying facts and opinions in short selections.

"Fat" (page 111): This article tells why fat is necessary in a healthy diet.

"Insects as Food" (page 113): This article discusses how various people around the world include insects in their everyday diets.

Selection Type
Science Articles

Comprehension Skill
Distinguish Fact from Opinion

Standards
Reading
• Distinguish fact from opinion in various texts.
• Demonstrate a basic understanding of culturally diverse written texts.

Science
• Describe how various systems work together to perform a vital function.
• Categorize organisms according to their roles in food chains.

VOCABULARY

Introduce the vocabulary words. Write the words on the board. Help students find a definition for each word. Have students use each word in a sentence.

"Fat"
  diets

"Insects as Food"
  nutritious   *entomology*
  appetizing   *granaries*
  morsels   *garnish*
  cuisine   *larvae*
  plentiful   *irresistible*

Fact or Opinion?

BEFORE READING

Tap Prior Knowledge
"Fat": Ask the students what they know about fat in their diet. Is fat good or bad for them?

"Insects as Food": Ask the students if they have eaten an insect. Do they know anyone who eats insects? If they had to eat insects for food, what kind would they most likely eat?

Skill to Emphasize
Review the section about distinguishing facts and opinions on page 97. Tell the students to look for facts and opinions in the two articles. Facts can be proven, but opinions cannot be proven.

DURING READING

Preview Text Features
Have the students look at the recipe in "Insects as Food." It is a narration of process, or a how-to. The subtitles hint at the information in each section of the article. Boldfaced words indicate vocabulary words.

Comprehending the Selection
You may wish to model how to distinguish between facts and opinions by asking: *Which statements can be proved? Which statements cannot be proved?*

AFTER READING

Reinforce the Comprehension Skill
Ask the students to identify some facts and opinions in the articles and explain how they decided which was which. Ask the students what the writer's purpose is in each article. How is the purpose aided by the use of opinions in the selection? In the "Fat" article, the writer is trying to convince the reader that fat in a diet is not necessarily a bad thing. In "Insects as Food," the writer is trying to convince the reader that insects can be a tasty and nutritious addition to one's diet.

Distribute copies of the Fact-Opinion Chart on page 124 to help the students organize the information. Then have them complete the chart for the two articles.

Assess
Have the students complete the activities for each selection.

WRITE ABOUT IT

Distribute another Fact-Opinion Chart to the students. Have them use the chart to plan a letter on an issue they have opinions about. After they complete the chart, have them write a letter that contains both facts and opinions.

Fact or Opinion?

 Read each paragraph. Then darken the circle by the best answer for each question.

Our solar system has one sun. We call it a solar system because the word *sol* means sun in Latin. There are at least eight other planets besides Earth that travel in orbits around the Sun. We say at least eight because that is how many we know of at this time. There might, in fact, be more beyond Pluto that we cannot see. Even if more planets are found, Earth is still the best planet.

1. Which of the following is an opinion in the paragraph?
   Ⓐ Our solar system has one sun.
   Ⓑ We call it a solar system because the word *sol* means sun in Latin.
   Ⓒ There are at least eight other planets besides Earth that travel in orbits around the Sun.
   Ⓓ Even if more planets are found, Earth is still the best planet.

Many geologists, or earth scientists, believe the seven continents were once one large continent. This idea is not a new one. A German scientist suggested this idea about sixty years ago, but the idea was laughed at by other scientists. When people look at the shape of the continents, they often think they might fit together. This is one part of the argument for a supercontinent. Another piece of evidence is matching fossils that have been found in Africa and South America. Also, tropical plant fossils have been found in Antarctica. The idea of floating continents is a very interesting one.

2. Which of the following is a fact in the paragraph?
   Ⓐ The continents are moving on plates.
   Ⓑ This idea is not a new one.
   Ⓒ The idea of floating continents is a very interesting one.
   Ⓓ Tropical plant fossils have been found in Antarctica.

3. Which of the following is an opinion in the paragraph?
   Ⓐ A German scientist suggested this idea about sixty years ago.
   Ⓑ Matching fossils have been found in Africa and South America
   Ⓒ The idea of floating continents is a very interesting one.
   Ⓓ None of the above

Nonfiction Comprehension: Grades 5–6, SV 8948-6

Name _____ Date _____

➡️ **Read each paragraph. Then darken the circle by the best answer for each question.**

What is the history of the bicycle? In 1817, a contraption was invented that had two wheels but no pedals. It was a funny-looking machine. The rider pushed himself along on it. Then, about 25 years later, pedals were added. The first U.S. patent for a bicycle was given in 1866. This bicycle was nicknamed the "boneshaker" because it shook the rider around so much. It probably could break a bone or two in the rider. A really fast bike had a front wheel as tall as a man and a small back wheel. Finally, two wheels that were the same size were used, and a chain was added. Many other improvements, including air-filled tires, gears, and brakes, were made as the years went by. Now, the bicycle is a wonderful machine. Everyone should have one.

4. Which of the following is an opinion in the paragraph?
   Ⓐ In 1817, a contraption was invented that had two wheels, but no pedals.
   Ⓑ It was a funny-looking machine.
   Ⓒ Then, about 25 years later, pedals were added.
   Ⓓ The first U.S. patent for a bicycle was given in 1866.

5. What purpose do you think the writer used to write this article?
   Ⓐ personal
   Ⓑ literary
   Ⓒ persuasive
   Ⓓ informative

Coffee is a popular drink in the United States. It is made from the seeds of the coffee plant. These seeds are called coffee "beans" because they look like beans. Coffee is grown in a warm climate because it cannot stand any frost at all. Most coffee plantations are in South or Central America. Coffee contains the drug caffeine, which is a stimulant. It is called a stimulant because it increases body activity. Many people drink coffee to wake themselves up in the morning.

6. Which of the following is an opinion in the paragraph?
   Ⓐ Coffee is made from the seeds of the coffee plant.
   Ⓑ Most coffee plantations are in South or Central America.
   Ⓒ Coffee contains the drug caffeine, which is a stimulant.
   Ⓓ None of the above

Fat

Everyone talks about low-fat **diets**, but did you ever wonder why fat is important to your body? Did you know that your body stores fat and then turns it into energy?

Although some people think that you don't need fat, they're wrong! You get almost forty percent of your energy supply from fat. Your body even uses small amounts of fat for repairing cells. Fats do something else. They make food tasty and more filling.

Your body uses fat in many ways. Fat covers important body organs. If you get hurt, a layer of fat can protect you. Fat also acts as insulation by keeping body heat in. Fat can keep you alive. If you were without food for a very long time, your body would burn the stored fat for energy.

After fat enters your bloodstream, it is carried to fat cells throughout your body. When your body needs energy, it breaks up the fat so it can go through the fat cell walls and back into the bloodstream. The blood then takes the fat cells to where the energy is needed. Oxygen from the air we breathe helps to burn the fat. Energy is released into muscle cells, which help you throw a ball, ride a bike, or do any other activity. An extra potato chip or two never hurt anybody.

⬤➡ **Write a short paragraph to convince someone that fat is good for you. Write complete sentences. Use both facts and opinions in your persuasion.**

_____

_____

_____

_____

_____

_____

_____

_____

_____

Nonfiction Comprehension: Grades 5–6, SV 8948-6

Name _____ Date_____

Comprehension Review

 Darken the circle by the best answer.

1. Where does fat go after it enters your bloodstream?
   Ⓐ to muscle cells
   Ⓑ to fat cells
   Ⓒ to body organs
   Ⓓ to fat layers

2. What would probably happen if you eliminated all fat from your diet?
   Ⓐ You might harm your body.
   Ⓑ You would have more energy.
   Ⓒ You ride your bike faster.
   Ⓓ Your body heat would stay in better.

3. What would probably happen if you kept some fat in your diet?
   Ⓐ Your food might be tastier.
   Ⓑ You would feel weak.
   Ⓒ You would always be hungry.
   Ⓓ You would need insulation.

4. The main idea of this article is that ____.
   Ⓐ you should not eat any fat
   Ⓑ you should eat only fat
   Ⓒ some fat in your diet is good for you
   Ⓓ fat does not give you energy

5. What purpose do you think the writer used to write this article?
   Ⓐ personal
   Ⓑ literary
   Ⓒ persuasive
   Ⓓ informative

6. Which of the following is an opinion in the paragraph?
   Ⓐ You get almost forty percent of your energy supply from fat.
   Ⓑ An extra potato chip or two never hurt anybody.
   Ⓒ Fat also acts as insulation by keeping body heat in.
   Ⓓ Oxygen from the air we breathe helps to burn the fat.

7. Which statement is probably true about in-line skaters?
   Ⓐ They need less body fat than a walker.
   Ⓑ They need more body fat than a walker.
   Ⓒ They need about the same amount of body fat as a walker.
   Ⓓ They do not need to eat fat.

8. How does the author prove that fat is important in your diet?
   Ⓐ She tells you how fat goes to the bloodstream.
   Ⓑ She tells you how oxygen burns fat.
   Ⓒ She tells you the ways that fat helps your body.
   Ⓓ She tells you about tasty food.

Nonfiction Comprehension: Grades 5–6, SV 8948-6

Insects as Food

Believe it or not, most insects we see crawling on the ground or on our picnic blankets can be eaten. In fact, many bugs and insects are quite **nutritious**. Insects are low in fat and are good sources of protein. Insects can also be quite tasty if they are cooked properly. Many cookbooks feature insect recipes. There are even **entomology** newsletters and magazines devoted to insects as food.

You may not like the idea of eating a grasshopper or a beetle. But insects are probably better for you than the high-fat, high-salt, high-calorie diet that many people have today. Put down the fast food and get ready to pass the pest food!

What's That Fly Doing in My Soup?

Does the idea of eating creepy crawlers sound less than **appetizing** to you? Don't get scared, but did you ever notice tiny black specks in your cereal or bread? These might be flour beetles and other pests that live in **granaries**. They fall into the flour as the grain is being milled.

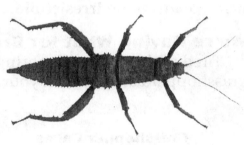

Did you ever notice tiny things flying around fruit in the market? Well, guess what they are. Fruit flies! Chances are you've been eating insects without even knowing it. Now that you have your feet wet, why don't you take the full plunge and taste a few delicious insect **morsels**?

If you'd like to try adding insects to your diet, it's important to know how to prepare them. What is the first step on the road to successful insect-eating? All insect food experts will tell you the same thing. Get the freshest insects you can find and cook them before eating them.

Insects usually are not found in supermarkets. However, you can purchase insects in pet stores or bait stores. You can also catch insects in the wild. Besides eating the whole insect, insect parts are also good to eat. You may want to begin by trying wings, legs, and eggs. Insects can make delicious main courses or make a lovely **garnish** for a festive holiday plate.

International Insect Snacks

Eating insects is not a new trend. In fact, people have been eating insects throughout history. Native Americans ate plenty of different insects long before Christopher Columbus came to America.

Today, many cultures around the world have insects in their **cuisine**. In fact, eighty percent of the world's population eats insects. In South America, people eat white beetles and ants. In Mexico, there is a particular ant that people use to make salsa. This ant is found only during the rainy season. In Algeria, people collect locusts in the desert, cook them in salt water, and dry them in the sunlight before eating them. In Japan, many insect items can be found on restaurant menus, such as boiled wasp **larvae** and fried grasshoppers with rice. People in West Africa eat termites and caterpillars.

Insects are not only tasty and nutritious, they are also **plentiful**. Yet why aren't people in America eating more insects today? The answer is simple. Many people think that insects are disgusting! You might agree, but imagine you were lost in the woods and it was getting dark. If you had to choose between starving and eating insects, what would you do? Who knows? You might find the crispy crunch of roasted ants to be **irresistible**.

We're Having What for Breakfast?

Tired of the same old, boring pancakes? Here's a simple and delicious recipe for grasshopper cakes to start your day right!

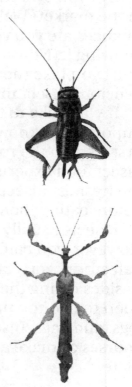

Grasshopper Cakes
- one egg
- twenty fresh, cooked grasshoppers
- two cups of cornmeal
- one teaspoon of cooking oil

1. Beat the egg in a bowl. Then add the grasshoppers and stir.
2. Put the grasshopper-and-egg mixture into a paper bag filled with cornmeal.
3. Make sure that the top of the bag is closed. Then shake the bag until the insects are completely covered with cornmeal.
4. Take the mixture out of the bag and make small pancake-size cakes, using your hands.
5. Ask an adult to help you fry the cakes in a skillet with a teaspoon of cooking oil. Drain and cool the cakes on a paper towel.
6. Serve plain or with syrup, butter, or honey.

Don't Let Insects Bug You!

Do you think you will be cooking buggy recipes anytime soon? If you do, remember that insects must be gathered and prepared properly. It's best to check with a health professional, a science teacher, or a parent before you take your first creepy, crawly, crunchy bite. Happy eating!

What Do You Think?

A fact is a statement that can be proven true. An opinion is someone's belief or feeling. A writer can include both facts and opinions in an article.

➤ **Use the article to fill in the fact–opinion chart. In the first column, write facts from the article. In the second column, write opinions from the article.**

Facts	Opinions
Most insects can be eaten.	Insect parts are also good to eat.
_____	_____
_____	_____
_____	_____
_____	_____
_____	_____

➤ **Use the fact–opinion chart above to answer each question. Write complete sentences.**

1. How does the writer feel about insects as food?

   _____

   _____

2. After reading the article, do you feel differently about eating insects? Explain.

   _____

   _____

   _____

   _____

Comprehension Review

 Write complete sentences to answer each question.

1. What would be another good title for this article?

   _____

   _____

2. What is the second step in making grasshopper cakes?

   _____

   _____

3. Why do you think the author wrote this article?

   _____

   _____

4. Why might insects be better for you than some of the foods you might eat regularly?

   _____

   _____

5. According to this article, how do people in Mexico use a particular ant in their food?

   _____

   _____

6. Do you think it is a good idea to eat insects? Explain.

   _____

   _____

   _____

   _____

   _____

Nonfiction Comprehension: Grades 5–6, SV 8948-6

Vocabulary Review

Darken the circle by the best answer.

1. In this article, *nutritious* means ____.
   Ⓐ unimportant
   Ⓑ good for the body
   Ⓒ delicious
   Ⓓ a type of insect

2. In this article, *entomology* means ____.
   Ⓐ the study of humans
   Ⓑ the study of insects
   Ⓒ the study of recipes
   Ⓓ the study of foods

3. In this article, *garnish* means ____.
   Ⓐ a main dish
   Ⓑ an insect from South America
   Ⓒ a small animal
   Ⓓ a piece of food used as a decoration

4. In this article, *morsels* means ____.
   Ⓐ large insects
   Ⓑ recipes
   Ⓒ small pieces of food
   Ⓓ small insects

5. In this article, *cuisine* means ____.
   Ⓐ a chef
   Ⓑ a style of cooking
   Ⓒ a type of insect
   Ⓓ a pancake

6. In this article, *larvae* means ____.
   Ⓐ insect bites
   Ⓑ ingredients
   Ⓒ young insects
   Ⓓ insect recipes

Build Your Vocabulary

Look for root words to help you understand the meanings of unfamiliar words.

Draw lines between the two columns to match each root word with the correct vocabulary word. Then write the definition of each vocabulary word on the line next to it.

7. appetite   irresistible _____

8. grain   plentiful _____

9. resist   appetizing _____

10. plenty   granaries _____

Nonfiction Comprehension: Grades 5–6, SV 8948-6

Name _____ Date_____

Main Idea Maps

Details

_____
_____
_____
_____

_____
_____
_____
_____

Main Idea

_____
_____
_____
_____

_____
_____
_____
_____

_____
_____
_____
_____

Details

_____
_____
_____
_____

_____
_____
_____
_____

Main Idea

_____
_____
_____
_____

_____
_____
_____
_____

_____
_____
_____
_____

Name _____ Date _____

Summary Chart

Important Idea

_____
_____
_____
_____

Important Idea

_____
_____
_____
_____

Important Idea

_____
_____
_____
_____

Summary

_____
_____
_____
_____
_____
_____
_____
_____
_____
_____
_____
_____
_____
_____

Nonfiction Comprehension: Grades 5–6, SV 8948-6

Name _____ Date_____

Sequence Charts

Event 1
_____
_____
_____

Event 2
_____
_____
_____

Event 3
_____
_____
_____

Event 4
_____
_____
_____

Event 1
_____
_____
_____

Event 2
_____
_____
_____

Event 3
_____
_____
_____

Event 4
_____
_____
_____

Nonfiction Comprehension: Grades 5–6, SV 8948-6

Name _____ Date_____

Cause

Effect

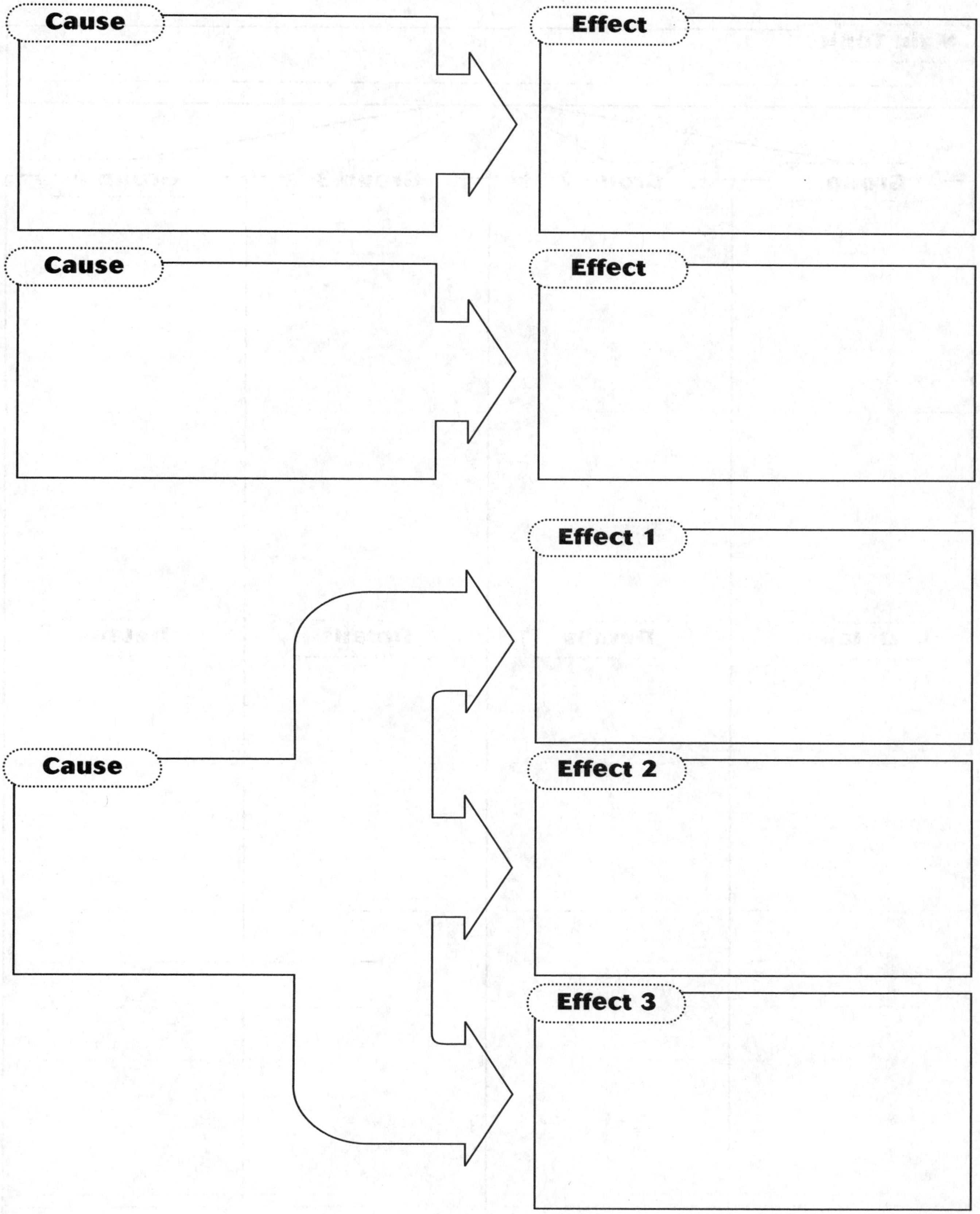

Cause

Effect

Cause

Effect 1

Effect 2

Effect 3

Blackline Masters: Cause-Effect
Nonfiction Comprehension: Grades 5–6, SV 8948-6

Name _____ Date_____

Classification Tree Diagram

Main Topic
_____
_____

Group 1   **Group 2**   **Group 3**   **Group 4**

Details   **Details**   **Details**   **Details**

Venn Diagram

Both

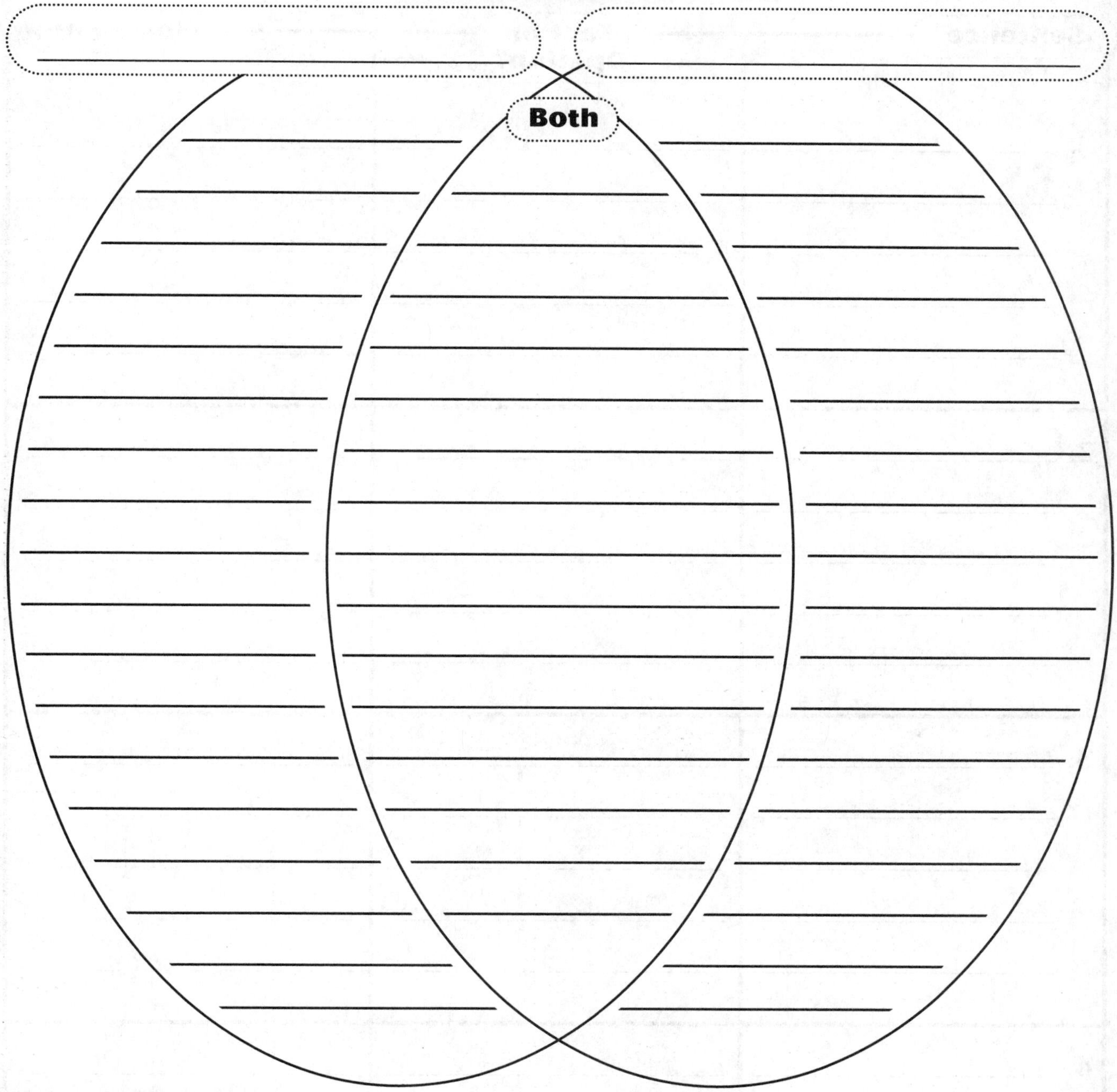

Main similarities:

_____

_____

Main differences:

_____

_____

Name _____ Date _____

Fact-Opinion Chart

Sentence	Fact or Opinion?	How I Know
1.		
2.		
3.		
4.		

Blackline Masters: Fact-Opinion
Nonfiction Comprehension: Grades 5–6, SV 8948-6

Page 7
1. 145
2. 55
3. 190

Diagram: The students' Venn diagram should have two interlocking circles, one labeled Horses, with 150 in the circle; the other should be labeled Pigs, with 100 in the circle. In the interlocking part of the circles should be 25. Outside the circle should be the label Farms, with 75.

Page 9
Correct order: 2, 3, 5, 1, 4, 6
1. C
2. B
3. D
4. B
5. All food chains start with plants because plants make their own food.

Page 11
1. A
2. A
3. C
4. A

Page 12
1. The North had the larger population.
2. The North had businesses that were more valuable.
3. The Union Army had 474,559 more soldiers than the Confederate Army.
4. Answers may vary. Possible response: The North was stronger at the beginning of the Civil War because it had more soldiers, a larger population to support the war effort, and more valuable businesses to produce supplies for the war.

Page 13
1. b
2. d
3. a
4. e
5. Answers may vary. Possible response: The populations of the North and South were different because the North had a much larger population and far fewer slaves.

Page 16
1. D
2. B
3. A
4. B
5. C
6. A
7. Answers will vary but should include details about one of the ten amendments in the Bill of Rights.

Page 17
1. A
2. B
3. C
4. D

Page 18
1. B
2. D
3. B
4. D

Page 20
1. Answers will vary but must include five of these states: Texas, Oklahoma, Kansas, Nebraska, South Dakota, North Dakota, Montana, Wyoming, Colorado, New Mexico.
2. The four major rivers that run through the Great Plains are the Canadian River, the Arkansas River, the Platte River, and the Missouri River.
3. Two physical features shared by places in this region are flat plains and low hills.
4. The climate in the Great Plains is dry, with very hot summers and very cold winters.

Page 21
1. C
2. D

Page 22
1. Answers will vary but must include three of these states: California, Oregon, Washington, Idaho, Montana, Wyoming, South Dakota, Colorado, Arizona, New Mexico, Alaska, Hawaii.
2. Old evergreen forests grow in the Northwest part of the United States.
3. The main trees in the Southeast part of the United States are pines and oaks.
4. Answers will vary according to state.
5. Few trees are found on the Great Plains because the climate is too hot and dry.

Pages 25–26
1. C
2. B
3. B
4. A
5. A
6. Answers may vary. Possible response: The details tell many unhappy things about his life.
7. B
8. Answers may vary. Possible response: The details tell many uses of seashells.
9. Answers may vary. Possible response: The Mississippi River is the major river in the United States.

Page 30
1. C
2. A
3. D
4. B
5. Answers may vary. Possible response: A spelunker must tie a knot correctly to be safe and not fall.
6. Answers may vary. Possible response: Cave animals are unusual because they live underground and prefer cold air and darkness.

Page 31
1. B
2. D
3. C
4. D
5. A
6. B
7. stalactites: thin pieces of rock that hang down from the roof of a cave
8. spelunking: the hobby of exploring caves
9. stalagmites: thin pieces of rock that stick up from the floor of a cave

Page 32
Chart: Details will vary. Possible responses: You may see amazing rocks. You may see bubbling streams and huge lakes. You may see unusual animals.
1. Answers will vary depending on the paragraph chosen.
2. Answers will vary depending on the paragraph chosen.

Pages 34–35
1. D
2. B
3. B
4. A
5. Alligators and crocodiles lay their eggs on land.
6. Alligators and crocodiles eat fish or small animals.
7. You can tell an alligator from a crocodile because they have different head shapes and the crocodile has two lower teeth that show when it closes its mouth.

Page 37
1. The German submarine sank the *Lusitania* with two torpedoes.
2. The *Lusitania* sank in about 15 minutes.
3. The passengers were eating lunch when the ship was attacked.
4. The *Lusitania* sank off the Irish coast about 10 miles from the Old Head of Kinsale.

Page 38
1. C
2. B
3. C
4. B
5. D
6. B
7. C
8. B

Page 40
1. B
2. A
3. D

Page 42
1. B
2. C
3. D
4. A
5. D
6. D
7. B
8. C

Page 43
Important ideas from each paragraph will vary.

Summaries will vary. Possible response: Sojourner Truth was the most important African American woman of her time. She was born as a slave in 1797, and her real name was Isabella. She had a sad life as a slave, and finally she ran away. She gained her freedom in 1828 and decided to use her life to fight injustice. She believed that all people were equal, and she helped African Americans to find better lives. When she died, many people were sad.

Page 46
1. B
2. B
3. D

Page 48
1. A
2. C
3. D
4. A

Steps will vary. Possible response: After studying math, science, and history, Blackwell was a teacher for a while. Then she began to study medical books and was taught by a doctor. She applied to many medical colleges, but she was not accepted. Finally, she was accepted and graduated in 1849. After working in Europe as a doctor, she returned to New York. There, she was not accepted as a doctor by the male doctors, so she started her own hospital and medical school. She and her sister trained women to become doctors.

Page 51
1. D
2. B
3. A
4. B
5. B
6. D
7. B
8. C

Page 52
Sentences will vary but should include key events at each time.
11:40 P.M.: An iceberg struck the side of the ship, and the *Titanic* began to sink.
12:45 A.M.: The first lifeboat, half-empty, was lowered into the water.
2:00 A.M.: All the lifeboats were in the water. Many people were left on the ship.
2:18 A.M.: The ship sank completely, with the band still playing.
4:10 A.M.: The *Carpathia* arrived and began picking up people in the lifeboats.

Page 54
1. B
2. D
3. A

Page 55
1. .240
2. 21 hits
3. 9 hits
4. 20 hits
5. .400

Page 57
1. C
2. D
3. B
4. D
5. Summaries will vary. Possible response: In a power plant, flowing water or steam spins the blades of a turbine, turning a large coil of wire. The coil of wire spins rapidly and constantly through the magnetic field of a giant magnet inside a generator, never leaving the field. Together, the coil and the giant magnet make a strong, steady electric current.

Pages 59–60
1. A
2. D
3. B
4. D
5. C
6. D
7. C
8. B

Page 64
1. Tsunamis are caused by seismic disturbances deep within the ocean.
2. The waves caused by the disturbances grow as they move across the ocean, sometimes reaching 200 feet high and moving 500 miles an hour. When they strike land, they can cause flooding and widespread destruction.
3. The volcano that erupted on Krakatau destroyed much of the island and caused tsunamis that killed many people on neighboring islands.
4. The bay floor in Lisbon was exposed when the trough of a tsunami struck first, causing the bay water to be sucked out into the larger wave. When the wave crest arrived minutes later, the bay refilled with water, drowning many people.
5. The earthquake off South America in 1960 caused tsunami waves that went many directions in the Pacific Ocean. The huge waves caused widespread destruction on many Pacific islands, including Hawaii. Later, giant waves slammed into Japan, killing many.

Page 65
1. C
2. A
3. D
4. A
5. B
6. B
7. analyze
8. ominous
9. complex
10. disturbances

Page 68
1. C
2. D
3. B
4. C

Page 69
1. D
2. C
3. Cockroaches smell with their antennae.

Page 72
1. B
2. A
3. D
4. B
Descriptions will vary.

Page 73
1. B
2. A
3. C
4. A
5. C
6. B
7. D
8. C

Nonfiction Comprehension: Grades 5–6, SV 8948-6

Page 75
The three parts of the U.S. government are the legislative, executive, and judicial branches.

Page 76
1. B
2. C
3. D
4. B
5. A
6. C
7. A
8. B

Page 78
1. B
2. C

Correct order of food chain: 1, 4, 3, 2
Explanations of food chain steps will vary. Possible response: The plants make their own food using nutrients provided by the decomposers. The rabbit eats the plants. The hawk eats the rabbit. The hawk dies. Then the decomposers break down the remains of the hawk. The plants use the nutrients from the dead hawk to make food. The chain begins again.

Page 79
1. A
2. B
3. C
4. A
5. A
6. B
7. C
8. B

Page 83
1. C
2. B
3. B
4. D
5. The four germs discussed in the article are bacteria, protozoa, fungi, and viruses.
6. Fungi is the kind of germ that includes molds and mushrooms.
7. Answers will vary.

Page 85
1. C
2. A
3. A
4. B
5. A
6. D
7. Answers will vary. Possible response: If the Sun was an O star, all life on Earth would probably die because the planet would be too hot to support life.

Page 87
1. B
2. A
3. B
4. C
5. D
6. D
7. Answers will vary. Possible response: Natural resources should be conserved to keep prices down and to save the resources for use by future generations.

Page 88
Answers may vary slightly.
Natural Resources: farmland, oil, fish, water, trees
Human Resources: teacher, janitor, carpenter, designer, letter carrier
Capital Resources: camera, computer, telephone, paint store, desk

Page 90
1. Renewable and nonrenewable resources are both used by people and are both provided by nature.
2. Renewable and nonrenewable resources are different because renewable resources can be made again fairly quickly, but nonrenewable resources take millions of years to make again.
3. Many nonrenewable resources are important because they are used as fuel.

Page 92
1. B
2. A
3. C
4. D
5. Answers will vary but should include three of these powers: collect taxes; punish crimes; hold elections; have courts; borrow money.
6. Answers will vary but should include three of these powers: control foreign trade; declare war; make peace treaties; control trade between states; create post offices.
7. Answers will vary but should include three of these powers: make education laws; create local governments; control business within the state; make marriage laws; issue drivers licences.

Page 94
1. C
2. A
3. C
4. A
5. Answers will vary. Possible response: The main difference between a series circuit and a parallel circuit is that power is delivered differently to the devices in the circuit.
6. Answers will vary. Possible response: In a series circuit, all the lights would go out, so each bulb would have to be checked separately to see if it still works.

Page 96
1. primates
2. monkeys, apes, humans
3. gibbons, chimpanzees, orangutans, gorillas
4. gibbons
5. orangutans
6. chimpanzees, gorillas
7. gorillas
8. gibbons
9. chimpanzees
10. gibbons, orangutans
11. chimpanzees, gorillas
12. gorillas

Pages 99–100
1. C
2. C
3. D
4. D
5. D
6. C or D
7. D

Page 102
1. C
2. A
3. C
4. D
5. B
6. B
7. A
8. D

Page 106
1. B
2. D
3. B
4. D
5. Answers will vary but should include two of these places: Philippines; Iwo Jima; Guam; Hawaii.
6. Hiroshima and Nagasaki were destroyed by atomic bombs.
7. Pearl Harbor in Hawaii was a battle in the Pacific that occurred in an area that Japan did not control.

Page 107
1. d
2. c
3. e
4. a
5. b

Pages 109–110
1. D
2. D
3. C
4. B
5. C or D
6. D

Page 111
Paragraphs will vary but should include details from the article.

Page 112
1. B
2. A
3. A
4. C
5. C or D
6. B
7. B
8. C

Page 115
Chart answers will vary. Possible responses:
Facts: Insects usually aren't found in supermarkets.; In fact, people have been eating insects throughout history.
Opinions: Insects can make a delicious main course or a lovely garnish.; Chocolate covered insects are a perfect after-school snack.
1. Answers will vary. Possible response: The author feels that insects are nutritious and can be tasty if prepared properly.
2. Answers will vary.

Page 116
1. Answers will vary. Possible responses: Insects Are Good Food or Who Wants a Roachsicle?
2. Put the grasshopper-and-egg mixture into a paper bag filled with cornmeal.
3. Answers will vary. Possible response: The author wrote this article to inform and persuade readers about eating insects as food.
4. Insects are lower in fat and calories and are more nutritious than many of the foods people eat regularly.
5. Mexicans use a special kind of ant to make salsa.
6. Answers will vary. Possible response: Yes, eating insects is a good idea because they are very nutritious.

Page 117
1. B
2. B
3. D
4. C
5. B
6. C
7. appetizing: something that looks and smells good to eat
8. granaries: buildings for storing grain
9. irresistible: too tempting to resist
10. plentiful: existing in large amounts

Reference
Fountas, I.C. and G.S. Pinnell. 2001. *Guiding Readers and Writers: Grades 3–6.* Portsmouth, NH: Heinemann.